CREATIVITY
CULTURAL PERSPECTIVE

CREATIVITY

Cultural Perspective

Dr. Ashok K. Hota

M.A., Ph.D., Dip, E.V.G. (NCERT)
Dept. of Education
Sinapali College
Sinapali - 766 108
(Orissa)

Discovery Publishing House
New Delhi-110 002

First Published - 2000

Reprinted - 2017

ISBN: 978-81-7141-537-3

Creativity – Cultural Perspective

Published by:

DISCOVERY PUBLISHING HOUSE PVT. LTD.
4383/4B, Ansari Road, Darya Ganj
New Delhi-110 002 (India)
Phone: +91-11-23279245, 43596064-65
Fax: +91-11-23253475
E-mail: discoverypublishinghouse@gmail.com
sales@discoverypublishinggroup.com
web: www.discoverypublishinggroup.com

Printed at:
Infinity Imaging Systems
Delhi

Preface

It is a common sense that a personality mostly depends on one's biological inheretance and sociocultural stimulation, The inherited biological make-up coupled with socio-cultural conditions help one's creativity to blooms and prospers. Thus creativity is a potentiality of one's personality, flourishes best in a condusive socio-cultural environment. Creativity is also culture bound. Human behaviour, as Sapir (1934) corroborates to our theory, may be studied in terms of the culture of the groups as a whole and psychic organisation of the individual. The present study investigates the differences in verbal, figural and composite creativity in the contexts of urban, rural tribal cultural settings. The study also explores the gender difference (also inter group gender differences) of urban, rural and tribal groups. Achievement motivation and self concept of high and low creative and relationship between intelligence and creativity are also statistically analysed.

The book has all total six chapters. First chapter gives an introduction emphasising the need of the study from socio-cultural, guidance parental and educational stand points. Meaning and nature of creativity is discussed from different angles in second chapter. In third chapter Creativity is studied from cultural context. This includes review of related studies, study of creativity in urban, rural and tribal culture, gender differences in creativity indifferent cultural group etc. In chapter four, creativity is studied in relation to certain variables such as : Achievement Motivation, Self-concept and Intelligence. This includes review studies in connection with creativity and those related variables. In this chapter the relationship between creativity and intelligence is also analysed.

Development of creativity emphasising implications of research findings are presented in fifth chapter. The last chapter represents research needs highlighting the delimitation and recommendations for further research.

It is hoped that the book will prove to be quite useful to teachers, trainers students, planners, administrators, researchers as well as parents who are really concerned with the creative intelligence and cultural upsurgence.

A.K. Hota

Acknowledgements

The author wishes to express his gratitude to Dr.Mohan C.Naik, Bolangir Training College, Bolangir, Orissa for his constant supervision of my earlier research project entitled 'A Study of Creative Potential Achievement Motivation and self-concept of Urban Rural and Tribal Adolescents of Western Orissa' which ultimately come out in the present book form.

Thanks are also due to Prof. M.K. Raina, Dr. (Miss) Arunima Vats of National Council of Educational Research and Training (N C E R T) New Delhi. Late Prof. N.M. Bhagia of National Institute of Educational Planning and Administration (NIEPA) New Delhi, Prof. J.N. Joshi and Prof. (Miss) Gakhar of Punjab University, Chandigarh for their timely suggestions and advices during the preparation of this work.

A host of students besides many teachers including headmasters of different schools where from the data for the study were collected, helped a lot at various stages. Their number is too large to mention individually here but they shall ever be remembered gratefully for the valuable cooperation they rendered.

Author is thankful to Mr. Santosh Kumar Meher, Lecturer in Economics, Sinapali College, Sinapali who helped me correcting the typed manuscript carefully.

Author gratefully acknowledges the research support provided by ICSSR, Chandigarh and New Delhi in the shape of study grants during the period of the study without which the project work would not have been possible.

Lastly, the words of gratitudes are expressed to authors and publishers whose works have been freely referred to in the present work and also to Discovery Publishing House, New Delhi for publishing it so nicely.

A.K. Hota

Contents

Contents

List of Tables and Figures

Introduction

Introduction

It is essential that every nation should feel concerned about its potential human resources. It has been observed by specialists that a country shall not be able to sustain economic growth unless all the reserves of creative potential in population are actually sought out and attracted into the required educational channels. Further, if education to-day is to give something to our future citizen; it is not knowledge or information alone, nor the certificates nor even some of the practical skills which they develop and use in day-to-day problems of life; but a trained intellect which would enable them to adjust and readjust themselves in the fast changing world in which they live to-day. Creative thinking too, as has been shown, gets stultified when not properly cared for and stimulated (Mehdi, 1977). If deplorable waste of creative potential is to be prevented and if the creative and talented are not to choose the path of delinquency, mental illness or at best a life of mediocrity and unrealised potentialities, then it becomes essential that creative potential be identified and cultivated. Hence, the imperativeness of research work in the field of creativity so as to provide humanity with productive ideas to stimulated Creativity (Kothari Commission, 1966).

Significance of the Study

The importance of the study can be recognised by focusing light on different significant values given below:

Socio-Cultural Value

India, one of the largest countries of the world, contains about 97 crores of people speaking more than a dozen languages, following several religions, living in divers geographical climates and terrains. A majority of these people live in rural areas, some live in trial areas and comparatively a very small section lives in urban areas. Marked differences are observed among these urban, rural and tribal people on socio-economic standing, possibilities and incentives opened for them. Social interaction, child-rearing practices, social values and the sense of appreciation finally determines the socio-cultural values. The opportunities and incentives that one cultural group enjoys, may rove a limitation for another group or vice versa. The development of human abilities is the function of the constituent of the body or brain on the one hand and experiences and perceptions obtained from socio-cultural conditions on the other. Each culture, as Ross Mooney (1969) maintains, has a "logos". It is perhaps this "logos" which either acts as a catalytic force or as a deterrent to the development and expression of creativity. It is because of this logos that cultures differ in the specific activities which they encourage, stimulate and value. The higher mental process of one culture may be relatively worthless "stunts" of another (Anastasi, 1949). It is this logos that cultures differ in the specific activities which they encourage, stimulate and value. The higher mental process of one culture may be relatively worthless 'stunts' of another (Anastasi, 1949). It is this logos which provides for different models and different notions of creativeness stemming from varying intellectual and philosophical traditions. Child is the product of his bio-social inheritance. With the booming being of birth, the infant develops a style of life commensurate with the sanctioned norms of the culture he is born in. Creativity is culture bound. As has been mentioned earlier, a creative act in a culture, might well be non-creative in another. Anderson and Anderson (1969) who gathered data from a large number of children of eight countries found that there exists large and significant differences consistent with their hypotheses about the impact of culture on creativity. Emphasizing the prominence of culture from behavioural stand point Sapir (1934) writes, human behaviour may be studied in terms of culture of the group as a whole and psychic organization of the individual himself. and employment of culture and individual perspectives upon the same collected data.

Creative potential, averes Gorden (1961) seeks its maximal actualization within the environmental conditions characterised by psychological safety and psychological freedom, and socio-cultural influence. Attributing family role Stress and Strauss (1968) theorized that children's Creativity varies according to the degree to which the child family role requires conformity to conventional norms. Children from permissive background tend to be more independent, cooperative and creative than those with orthodox upbringing. Similar views have been expressed by Watson, Baldwin, Hattwick, Symond and Carpenter. Culture, elaborated and developed, makes creativity possible and in turn, is enriched by creativity. Discussing the importance of culture in nurtunance and development of creative potential, Rollomay (1969) very succinctly observed that you can never localize Creativity as a subjective phenomenon, you can never study it in terms of what goes on a person ..... For what is occurring is always a process, a doing, specifically a process interrelating the person and his world.

Such are the powerful influences of culture in the promotion of creative development and functioning. It is because of these influences that the nature and number of creative productions showed great variations among the cultures (Krosber, 1944). Since culture has such a pronounced role in the development of creativity. The understanding and study of culture win relation to this important functioning has its own right for research. Perhaps, it is because of this. E. Paul Tolerance has pointed out that comparative studios of creativity in children have a promise in pointing the way to the creation of conditions that would produce healthier more creative people.

Guidance Value

Creativity, like intelligence, significantly influences the school accomplishment. Very recently Yadav (1987) reported that academic achievement is remarkably correlated with creativity. It is only because of this realization, in most of the talent search examinations; the use of creativity measures are being increasingly felt now-a-days.

Guidance workers or school counsellors helping students in educational problems generally use the intelligence measure but their growing awareness in the area of creativity suggests them to employ creativity measures also in solving educational problems. It is perhaps because of this creativity measures (TTCT). asserted Swess (1981), should be used in students for educational guidance.

Understanding and helping the students in relation to any behaviour, comprising creativity and intelligence, requires the study of their socio-cultural background; because abilities develop in relation to physical constituent of the individual and the practices and experiences acquired from socio-cultural environment to which the individual is exposed.

Since the concept of creativity is such an important phenomenon, its proper study requires a comparative research taking urban, rural and tribal culture into account with its other related variables like achievement motivation and self-concept.

Parental Value

Parents need to recognise and understand the role of socio-cultural factors in developing and shaping human abilities including Creativity. Parents should realise the fact that poor quality of schooling coupled with disadvantageous home background accentuates the effect of socio-cultural and academic deprivation that has a detrimental effect on verbal and non-verbal creative thinking abilities (Ahmad and Joshi, 1978). Some cultural conditions are favourable for certain abilities whereas others are inimical to those. Early childhood experiences including child rearing practices, parent-child interaction parental treatment, their values, attitude, parental role expectancy of children, custom and tradition go a long way to provide environment which fosters or stifles creativity in children.

The wide cultural differences in the form of urban, rural and tribal regions and sex role promotion in the form of male or female or son or daughter represented in creative potential achievement motivation and self-concept of the children is evident from a number of studies. Hence, the need of the present study is equally recognised for parental value.

Educational Value

Creativity at its highest level has probably been as important as any human quality in changing history and in shaping the world (Taylr, 1964). Environment exerts a great influence upon the child. The school where he spends a considerable time and gets formal education assumes importance in shaping his abilities (Sharma, 1979). Creativity can be fostered within the individuals by providing enriched academic environment. Education can do a great in promoting creative performance, if perhaps not in production the abilities themselves. But the education is too bookish and mechanical. Stereotyped and rapidly uniformed that it does not cater to the different aptitudes of pupils. The stress on examination, the over crowded syllabus, the method of teaching and lack of proper material amenities tend to make education a burden rather than a joyous experience to the young mind (Secondary Education Commission, 1952-53) and naturally does very little to exploit the value potential of individuals. Already faced with alarming rate of wastage and stagnation and problems like 'Mass illiteracy', 'brain-drain', and 'malnutrition' no one can simply close his eyes to the tremendous lapse that results in our failure to identify and develop, in our youth, the limit of their creative potential. This point has also been emphasized in the report of Education Commission (1966) which says, 'Even the talent that enters schools and succeeds in climbing the educational ladder does not flourish fully because it has not discovered sufficiently early, and is often studying in poor school.

It is a fact that creativity like other personality traits is distributed normally in the population and there is every possibility to be creative in one's own field. But here it would be apt to quote Stoddard (1959) in this connection that the urge to inquire, to invent, to perform is stifled in millions of school children, now growing up, who do not get above rate learning or atleast do not stay about it. Likewise Osborn (1963) says that the organization of our schools, our curriculum or text books pay homage to same God of conformity, even the selection system in education emphasises convergent abilities.

Recognising, understanding and valuing creativity from socio-cultural context is much more important as socio-cultural conditions favour or hamper creativity in the young children. The disadvantaged children have a significantly-low Creativity score in comparison to their advantaged counterparts (Singh, 1980). However, optimistically Sultana (1980) viewed that socio-cultural disadvantage readers the development of both verbal and non-verbal Creativity but the deficiency can be overcome by a quality education. From educational stand point it is a matter of vital importance that better environment be provided to children to blossom and it is here that the role of the teachers in helping to foster creativity among school going children needs to be emphasized most (Badrinath and Satyanarayan, 1978-79). Hence, Research work in this area will be quite informative, stimulating and promising.

Statement of the Problem

Based on the above theoretical considerations the present research problem was, therefore, stated as under :

> "A STUDY OF THE CREATIVE POTENTIAL ACHIEVEMENT MOTIVATION AND SELF-CONCEPT OF URBAN, RURAL AND TRIBAL ADOLESCENTS".

2

Creativity : Theoretical Framework

Introduction

The present chapter is devoted to concept of Creativity. The meaning, nature and concept of Creativity is discussed from the following points of view :

i) Creativity - a global view
ii) Guilford's Multivariate view
iii) Associative concept of Creativity
iv) Creativity and Intelligence

Creativity: A Global View

As a result of extensive work carried out during the past two decades or so the concept of Creativity has become important, sometimes almost a cult in educational and psychological thinking. Even the most perfunctory semantic analysis, however, suggests that the concept of Creativity commonly employed is amorphous and indefinite. Creativity as a concept has different meanings and inter-pretations for different people. It is a construct not easy to define because it is a multifaceted phenomenon. At one place Guilford observed 'Creativity' like love is a many splendoured thing. Agreeing substantially with Guilford, Mackinnon (1970) explains, many are the meanings of Creativity, for most it denotes the ability to bring something new into existence while for others it is not an ability but the psychological processes by which novel or valuable products are fashioned. For still others, Creativity is not the process but the product. Definitions of Creativity range all the way from the notion that Creativity is simple problem solving to conceiving it as the full realization and expression of an individual's unique potentialities....Since Creativity properly carries all these meaning and many more besides, it is indeed a multifaceted phenomenon, But despite the fact that concept of Creativity is so amorphous it is also highly useful.

Traditionally, Creativity was considered a rare mysterious phenomenon non blessed with define inspiration, occurring mainly in a few outstanding geninses such as Devinci, Mozart, Einstein or Helmhdtz, although it was realized that many other generally more mediocre artists or scientists produced occasional or minor creative work. The current trend, however, is to see Creativity as speed through almost the entire population. In response to the question - Are there any non-creative people ? Murphy optimistically writes, "We know from watching children in progressive schools that the desire to create must be almost universal; and that almost every one has some measure of originality which stems from his fresh perception of life and experiences from the uniqueness of his own fantasy when he is free to share it." Supporting Murphy, Louis Flieglerl says, 'Individuals are creative in divers ways and to different degree....Creativity is within the realm of individual depending upon the area of expression and capacity of the individual.

As stated earlier, there are many definitions of Creativity, each stressing one or the other aspect, like - person, process, product and press.

Creativity is, sometimes, thought to be an attitude of mind. Creative persons are distinguished from non-creative ones, by interests, attitudes, values, motive and drive (Dellas and Gaier, 1970). In order to identity creative talent psychologists do stress on personality characteristics and motivational aspects including needs, attitudes, values rather than only intelligence, achievement and aptitudes which to some extent also help the individual to be productively creative (Hudson, 1936; Burt, 1962; Bloom, 1963; Guilford, 1967; Dellas and Gaier, 1970). Adopting an extreme view Hudson (1966) suggested that roots of creativity do not seem to lie in convergent or divergent thinking, but rather in personality and motivational aspect of character. Osbern (1971) classifies creative energy into two main types — emotional and volitional, though they cannot be clearly separated. Therefore, the driving power must come from our feelings and will. Easton too agrees that creative thinking is not purely an intellectual process but is dominated by emotions from start to the finish. Elliott synthesizing the writings of Maslow, Rogers and Assagiots takes the liberty to suggest that their metaphors of creativity are volitional in orientation. They view creative act as the product of will.

Certain personal qualities help the individual to be creative in his own field. Rogers (1961) believed that certain conditions and personal characteristics within an individual area associated with creativity: Opennass (descriptive terms like adventuresomeness, inquisitiveness), internal locus of evaluation (ascribing success as a result of efforts and self-confidence), and ability to toy with elements. Review of published work in the area of creativity reveals that the qualities are risk-taking independence in making judgement, less authoritarian, accepting chances, persistence (Stein and Heniza), awareness of other, humour, non-conformist, confidence, self sufficiency, accepting disorder, strong affection (significant characteristics out of 84 personality traits, Torrance, 1968), fluency, flexibility, originality and elaboration in thinking, scepticism , intellectual playfullness (Guilford 1973), in the realm of scientific creativity the role of self-confidence and risk-taking (Kalpan, 1963); risk taking both to the creative person and to the creative act (Barron, 1963); individual's capacity to generate a number of associates to creative tasks and preferred level of risk (Pankove & Kogan, 1968). strong achievement motivation (McClelland, 1963) and many more characterises creative persons at all level whether they are in school or have grown into adults. But it is a fact that the personality qualities of creative writer may differ from the personality characteristics of a creative scientist or a creative mathematician as their specific fields differ from one another (Hota, 1984).

In the "Dictionary of Education" C.V. Good described Creativity as associational and ideational fluency with originality, spontanity, flexibility adoptability and ability to make more original evaluation. Creativity, sometimes, appears to be a process involved in problem solving. In his book Guiding Creative Talent, Torrance defined it at "becoming sensitive to problems, difficulties, gaps in knowledge, missing element, search for new solution, making guesses, hypotheses and finding new ways". He further claims that under this definition, it is possible to subsume the major elements of most other definitions. Torrance's definition lists four ways in which people behave creatively. The first behaviour is the process of sensing difficulty, being aware of the problems or missing elements in information. This is an evaluative thinking process. The second behaviour is that of formulating hypotheses, making guesses, asking questions, investigating and manipulating information. This is the divergent thinking process which consists of the abilities of being fluent, flexible, original and elaborating. The third is another evaluative process which calls for testing and revising hypotheses, guesses, questions, Here again the mental abilities of setting criteria, judging, modifying, resting and remaining flexible come into play. The last behaviour is communicating the results to others. On the same line Yamamoto (1964) defined creativity as the process of formulating new ideas or hypotheses, testing these ideas or hypotheses and communicating the results.

Analysing the thought process of Helmhdtz the famous German physicist and poincare, the great mathematician, Grahm Wallas (1926) concluded four distinct stages in creative thinking. They are: preparation, incubation, illumination and verification. Although, some writers have introduced changes in the nomenclature (Nash, 1966) and a few others have broken them into more divisions, the four stages enumerate by Wallas receive wide acceptance. Preparation is the first stage during which the problem is viewed and analysed from different angles. During incubation ideas of evaluation go under ground and become unconscious. During the third stage, illumination, the individual expresses a flash of light and suddenly gets the solution of his problems. Finally comes the stage of verification when the original idea or hypothesis is tested, if necessary, reviewed. Unlike the preceding two stages over this stage our conscious 'will' has comparatively full control (Wallas, 1926). Wallas (1926) and Motamedi (1983) provide excellent models for understanding experience of creative persons. Motamedi expands the model to include seven passages - framing, probing, exploring, revelating, affirming, refraining and realizing. Taking the conscious and subconscious mind into account. Spearman (1930) defined 'creativity' "basically a process of sensing or creating relationship with both conscious and subconscious process operating".

Mednick (1962) defines creative thinking as "....the forming of associative elements into new combinations which either meet specified requirements or in some way useful." Wallach and Kogan (1965) accepting Mednick line, have defined creativity, most appropriately, refers to the ability to generate or produce with some criticism of relevance, many cognitive associates that are unique. Believing on the S.R. association Wallach and Kogan are of the opinion that it is the creative ability which prompts the individual to produce a number of associations to a particular stimulus and some unique responses in the form of fluency and originality respectively. According to him a creative person having more fluency can generate large number of associations and a creative person having originality produces some unique, uncommon, new and original responses. Perhaps, their own definition was the criterian for developing the wallach-Kogan test of Creativity.

Another aspect of creative process which seems to have been much debated among the psychologists is the source of creative ideas. Vernon (1972), analysing the introspective reports of different creative individuals, finds that all of them refer to ideas coming to them from outside the realm of the conscious thought. So far as this finding points to the important role of non-conscious process in creative thinking there cannot be any doubt about it. As was indicated earlier, during the stage of incubation the individual is working at the non-conscious level. But the point to be considered here is what that non-conscious level is? Authorities seem to differ on this point. Some writers (Ghiselin, 1952; Poincare, 1972) have identified this level with the 'unconscious' while others (Nash, 1966 and others) have held it to be the 'super conscious' which lies above the conscious level. Still others (including Kubie) believe that creative ability is predominantly a 'pre-conscious' process.

The author of the Mind's Best Work, D. Parkin (1983) makes clear his cognitive metaphor by insisting that creative activity is simply another form of thinking the kind of thinking involved in the solution of problems or the creation of product. Parkin's metaphor departs from earlier psychoanalytic metaphors which claims that creative behaviour is unconscious behaviour. As a result of Parkin's analytic scrutiny of creative individual, speaking aloud their creative process, he concludes that the work of practising artists reassembles the kind of work we engage in on a daily basis. This work consists of making plans, revising them, noticing gruities and sharing them with others (Gardiner, 1984). Prficient artists simply perform their work with more speed and facility than the average person.

Watching Creativity from somewhat different angle as Howard Gruber pointed out else where that being creative is not a state of mind one assumes when pursuing a specific artistic or intellectual task. It is an ever present activity. It is a life long process. It is a way responding to life (Steiner, 1985).

Morgan (1953) listed twenty five definitions of Creativity and viewed that creativity involves the development of something unique. The sculpture made by an artist, poetry composed by a poet breaks the conformity and traditionality in its content may be called creative activity or creative product. Essentially creative ability is an input to the creative process and the out-puts of creative process are products such as scientific papers, artistic drawings, musical compositions, report, devices such products vary in their innovationeness and productiveness. The uniqueness of the product also implies originality. The products germinates new possibilities which others may then develop or modify. To explain it further, highly innovative outputs (creative products) open new possibilities for research, development or utilization. Productive outputs on the other hand permit significant advancement along established line (Ban David, 1960).

Man, Louis A. Flieger maintains, during his creative act manipulates external symbols or objects to produce unusual event uncommon to himself and his environment (Kneller, 1965). Indeed, novelty or originality or uncommonness has been recognised by almost all authors as an essential element of creativity. Every creative act, it has been held, lead to novel product. But this definition of creativity, to be sure, cannot satisfy everybody. One would like to question further whether novelty or uniqueness is the sole requirement for an act or a product to be called creative? Guilford (1973), while putting his informational theory, writes "creativity suggests, recognise creative people and their creative products, some of which have social values." Thus, social value may be thought to be another criterion for creativity though the presence of the phrase, 'some of which' in Guilford's proposition places a question mark against any such generalization. To make it further clear-cut, Hein (1966), for the purpose of his research, defined creativity as that process which results in a novel work that is accepted as tenable or useful or satisfying by a group at some point of time. In fact the element of usefulness in creativity has been advocated by other researchers too (e.g. Mednick, 1962; Parnes, 1967). Unlike Burt and many others who intended to make a distinction between useful and useless creativity or good or bad creativity. Rogers did not consider it worthwhile to make any such distinction for two reasons. The fluctuating nature of social valuation of what is good and what is bad, and the other that many times creative products go unnoticed by the society. He also does not want to distinguish between different degrees and level of creativeness as done by Ghiselin (1966) and many others. According to Rogers, the action of the child inventing a new game with his playmates, Einstein formulating a theory of relativity, the house wife devising a new sauce for the meat, a young author writing his first novel, all of these are creative, and there is no attempt to set them in order of more or less creative (Rogers, 1959). Indeed, Rogers does not find any mental differences between different creative acts - be it painting, a picture, devising new instrument for killing or developing scientific theory. Thus, Rogers, view of creativity does away with the notion that creativity is confined to some field or only to people like Mozarat and Davinci or Gaillio and Newton, who would come in the extreme top of the population say one or two in a thousand. Creativity on the contrary is normally distributed trait to be found in all individuals across divers fields of creativity - Art, Science, literature, technology and even salesmanship (Kneller, 1965; Varvalin, 1971).

The uniqueness or originality of the product generates different interpretations by different authorities. Very recently, Wolff (1981) writes; to us to-day originality lies more in the imaginative ability to do something dramatically different (regardless of its intrinsic merits) or in the knack of inventing something out of whole cloth......Duer's originality, however, lies in one's ability to perceive and to transmit a particularly full and clear image of physical reality directly to paper by means of line and colour and without following certain rules for drawing based on centuries of tradition.

Newness is sometimes interpreted as renovated or rejuvenated or regenerated. Isaac Newton says 'if I have been able to see farther than others, it is because I have stood on the shoulders of gaints.....the creative writers, however, not only translates the messages across time from the foreign language of the past, he also adds new meaning with fresh insight, he revitalizes the storeis of the past. He creates it for the present.

From the stand point of new as unique or personal, Wolff (1981) writes - originality is more a matter of being than of doing, and exists in the vary nature of the individual who expresses it. It is intrinsic to identify and on its most primitive level is quite simply an individual's uniqueness. But creative product must go beyond new. It must also be of value.

A peep into the creativity literature reveals that creativity is seen not only as a person, as a process, as a product but it sometimes results from the person and his interaction with the environment which is known as 'press'. Describing creativity as a person, as a product and as a press, Rogers (1959) says: Creativity as an emergence in action of a noval relational product, growing out of the uniqueness of the individual on one hand and the material events, people and circumstances of his life on the other.

Those who consider creativity as stems from personal and environmental interaction are Barron, Botuinck, Craig, Damm, Dinkmayer and Caldwell, Gowan and Torrance, Guilford, Holland, Mooney and Rhodes etc. Parnes and Noller (1973) recorded dramatic gain in creativity of the individuals under favourable conditions of high motivation, appropriate training and encouraging environment. Koch, an American poet, was able to turn Ghetto children into budding poets by creating a relaxed, informal but highly stimulating environment (Good 1976). Here again environment is seen from two standpoints; Psychological and physical.

Humanistic psychologists consider creativity a naturally evolving component of 'psychological health'. According to them creativity is not the pessimistic avoidance of anxiety through fantasy, but rather the process of direct and deliberate confrontation between self and environment. The humanistic construct, unlike psychoanalytic, sees creativity as depending upon causes, occurring solely in childhood but also those actualized in present experiences. Ascribing the significance of psychological environment Rogers (1962) views that creativity is encouraged by a milieu of 'psychological safety' and 'psychological freedom'. Psychological safety, according to him, may be established by three associative processes such as (i) accepting the individual unconditionally, (ii) providing a climate in which external evaluation is absent, (iii) understanding empathetically. Regarding psychological freedom, Rogers points out that when a teacher, therapist or any other facilitating person permits the individual a complete freedom of symbolic expression, creativity is fostered. The physical environment consists of many things including home and school climate. Lack of conformity in the family, autonomy allowed to the child by the parents, tolerating parents for different and diverse opinions encouraging divergent thinking in the child are some of the conditions of home atmosphere contributing to creative growth in children. Investigators like Crutch field (1962) and Cross (1966) strongly supported this view.

In teaching learning situation certain principles of teacher behaviour, Torrance views, can be very helpful in promoting the creativity of the students such as respect shown by the teacher for unusual questions of the students being respectful towards the imagination and unusual ideas of the students and valuing them, allowing the child to do something without the threat of evaluation (non-evaluative atmosphere). These principles and may more equally applicable to classroom teachers as well as parents in the family.

Weber (1967) produced evidences by students higher figural creativity scores that the figural creative potentialities of the pupiles may be developed more under the influence of consistent patterns of direct teacher behaviour. He further concluded that verbal higher creativity scores may be developed more under the influence of indirect patterns of teacher behaviour. Weber statements were also validated by Pandey's (1979) findings. With regards to originality, Khatena (1968) reported significant effect of different teaching strategies on originality dimension of creativity. Giving a sort of summer statement. Singh (1985) asserts that change in some characteristics of teacher behaviour develops creativity among school children.

Burgett (1982) tentatively presented some postulates whose revision and growth are dependent on the creative efforts of those who are devoted to recognizing and nurturing creativity within the academic community.

Creativity requires one exercise the ability to fashion continually fresh and new responses to problems presented by an available body of knowledge constitutes the first postulate which challenges the notion that restricts creativity to specific domains.

The second postulate narrates that creativity is the function of growth and growth is the function of human beings. Since all human being grow, all are creative. This postulate challenges the notion that creativity properly is the domain of an elite few.

Creativity requires imagination i.e. the ability to expand one's vision beyond the available body of knowledge. This third postulate is a challenge to the body of knowledge itself.

The next postulate requires courage....creativity appears to prosper, but in an environment which is both safe and congenial to such process. Courage is needed to reverse the process of being uncreative and to begin to reclaim the natural curiosity all humans possess at birth. Courage is needed to raise the individuals tolerance of ambiguity. Again, courage is needed to neutralize the fear which immobilizes most humans into behaving in ways that are mindless repetitive and which are irresponsible.

The last postulate states that creativity requires logical thinking and sensitive intuition which one executes with elegance. The human being intellect is perhaps its greatest creative asset. The human can choose to be logical....There is a distinction between thinking and feeling. Feelings are not rational phenomena, and while they may help to inform; reason they are, by themselves, not at all dependable guides to action in a rational, human sense (Jackins, 1973)). Thus the responsible human creator is one which is incharge of his/her feelings, is in charge of the logic which conforms the landscape of available alternatives, and is in control of and responsible for the decision which are made in response to these factors.

II
GUILFORD'S MULTIVARIATE VIEW OF CREATIVITY DERIVED FROM S I MODEL

The factor analysis studies of Guildford and his associates led to his three dimensional model entitled, "the Structure of Intellect". By ways of analysing thinking abilities, they have examined very carefully the factors beyond those generally associated with intelligence and reached the conclusion; we must look well beyond the boundaries of the I.Q. if we are to fathom the domain of Creativity.

In his presidential address to American Psychological Association in 1950, Guildord mentioned the hypothesis and assumption that were basic to his theory of "Structure of intellect."

Creativity represents patterns of primary abilities, patterns which can vary with different spheres of creative abilities. Each primary ability is a variable, along with individuals differing in a continuous manner. Consequently, the nature of those abilities can be studied in people who are not necessarily distinguished for creative response. Productivity depends upon primary traits, including interests, aptitudes and temperamental variables. It is suggested that certain kinds of factors will be found including sensitivity to problems, ideational fluency, analytical ability, recognition or redefinition ability. Span of ideation, structure and evaluation ability.

Guilford does not accept the concept of a unitary general intellectual ability or of a primary mental abilities. His model (1967 b) is foremost illustration of the systematic identification of specific intellectual abilities. Figure No. 2.1 diagrams 120 possible human abilities in the cognitive domain, most of which have been identified through tests (Guilford and Hoeptner, 1966; Hoeptner, Guilford and Bradley, 1968; Hoffman, Guilford, Hoeptner and Dohart y, 1968). Guilford (1967 b) defines an ability as 'a union of an operation, a content, and a product'. In his model of the "Structure of Intellect", there are five operations, four types of contents and six products; therefore, there are 5x4x6 = 120 abilities. On the basis of this, Guilford suggests that there can be 120 ways of being talented on the basis of 120 hypothesised factors. A brief overview of the operations, contents and products follows :

Operation

Operation indicates the mental process performed or activity involved. Major kinds of intellectual activities or processes, things that the organism does with the raw materials of information,

information being defined as "that which the organism discriminates."

C. Cognition : Immediate discovery, awareness, rediscover, or recognition of information in various forms; comprehension and understanding. Reading is a process, a complex activity involving many intellectual abilities.

M. Memory : It refers to retention of information. It is an important aspect of the intellect, as no content without retention be used at need, or at a later time. This operation represents the simple reproduction of facts, formulae or other items recognized and remembered contents through use of certain processes, like rote memory, selective recall, etc.

D. Divergent production : Generation of information from given information, where the emphasis is upon variety and quantity of out put from the same source. It is also called transfer. This operation is most clearly involved in aptitude of creative potential.

N. Convergent Production : Generation of information from given information, where the emphasis is upon achieving conventionally accepted best outcomes. It is likely the given (cue) information fully determines the response.

E. Evaluation : Reaching decision or making judgements concerning criterion satisfaction (correctness, suitability, adequacy, desirability, etc.) of information.

Contents

Content is a raw material to which mental process is applied. The broad classes or types of information iscriminable by organism are :

F. Figural: Figural content is concrete material as perceived through senses, like share, diagrams, sizes, etc. It is represented by geometric patterns and designs which does not convey intrinsic meanings, but have all extrinsic meaning information in concrete form. The term figural mainly implies figure ground perceptual organization. Visual spatial information is figural. Different sense modality may be involved e.g. visual, kinesthatic, etc.

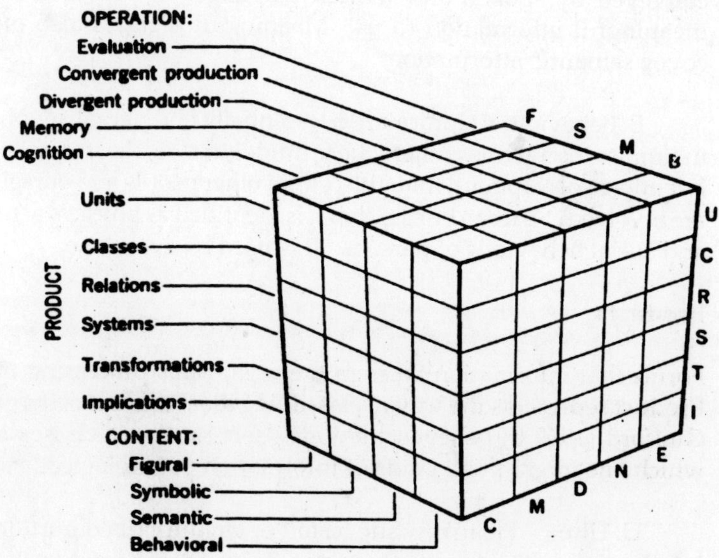

Fig. 2.1 Structure of Intellect Model

S. Symbolic: It is represented by letters or numbers or other conventional signs, which can act as members of some formula to convey some meaning. Its information is abstract, having no significance in themselves, such as letters, numbers, musical notions, when meanings and form are not considered.

M. Semantic: It takes the form of verbal meanings or ideas as conveyed by spoken and written language. It provides more meaningful information to us. Meaningful pictures also often covey semantic information.

B. Behavioural : Information, essentially non-verbal, involved in human interactions where the attitudes, needs, desires, moods, intentions, perceptions, thoughts, etc. of other people and ourselves are involved. So it can be said that it is identified as physical actions and social behaviour of persons. It is used by every one.

Products

Forms that information takes in the organism's processing of it. Product represents the way of classifying ideas and concepts or as Guilford (1959 b) believed they may serve as basic classes into which one might fit all kinds of information psychologically.

U. Untis: - Relatively suggested or circumscribed portion of information with a 'thing' character. Thus it is the product in the form of an individual item or thing. May be close to gestalt psychology's "figure on a ground".

C. Classes: - Conceptions underlying sets of items of information grouped by virtue of their common properties.

R. Relation: - Conneciion between units (items) of information, based upon variables that apply to them both. Relational connections are more meaningful and definable than implication. This relation may be between two or more items of positive or negative kind.

S. System: Organised or structural composite of items of information, having interacting or inter-related parts. It differs from a class in the manner that a class is not organised, and items are counted on the basis of common characteristics, but in a system the organization of items is the main key of consideration.

Transformation: Changes of various kinds (redefinition, shifts, or modification) of existing information or in its functions. It is thus a reinterpretation of an information.

Implication: Exploration of information in the form of expectancies, prediction, known or suspected, antecedents, concomitants, or consequences. The connection between the given information and that extrapolated is more general and less definable than a rational connection (Guilford and Hoeptner, 1966).

Guilford believed that factors contributing to creativity are related, particularly to the 'operational aspect' of intellect; viz; 'divergent production; categories. Initially he relates divergent thinking to certain well known ability factors (viz. fluency, flexibility, originality, and elaboration) which seem to go with creative output. Later on, he believed that redefinition abilities, which are 'converqent production' category, and sensitivity to problems which falls in the 'evaluation' category of his 'structure of intellect' are also important for creative activity.

There are 24 calls for divergent-production (DP) abilities as envisaged by 'Structure of Intellect' theory. Out of these 24,23 have been demonstrated (Guilford, 1970). Most of the areas of creation, as he maintains, could be counted by these abilities and following factors and tasks for assessing them may be regarded as summarizing Guilford's theory concerning the measurement of the thinking abilities involved in creativity (Guilford and Marrifield, 1960):

Factor	*Tests and Descriptions*
Sensitivity to problems (seeing defects, needs deficiencies, seeing the odd, the unusual; seeing what must be done).	*Apparatus Test* - Suggest two improvements for a common appliance. Seeing Problems - List problems that might arise in connection with common objects. *Seeing Deficiencies*- Point out the way in which a described plan or activity is faulty.
Figural Spontaneous Flexibility	*Cube Fluctuations* - Indicate the number of changes in perspective

Factor	*Tests and Descriptions*
	of ambiguous cube (Thurstone. *Windmill alternations* - Indicate the number of alternative from the illusion to another while observing shadow of rotating rectangular blade. (Thurstone) *Rational rivalry Reversals* : Indicate the number of reversals when a blue field is presented stereoscopically to one eye and a yellow field to the other eye. (Thurstone)
Figural Adaptive Flexibility	*Match Problems II* : Indicate three or four different patterns of a specified number of matches that can be removed to leave a specified number of triangles or squares. *Match Prolmes III*: Indicate several different patterns of matches that can be removed to leave a specified number of squares. Planning Air Maneurvers : Select the most different path in "skywriting" letter combinations. (USAF)
Word Fluency	*Suffixed W-1* : Write words ending with a specified suffix (ETS) Prefixed W-2: Write words beginning with a specified prefix. (ETS). First and last letters W-3: Write words beginning and ending with a specified letters. (ETS).
Expressional Fluency	*Expressional Fluency* : Write four word sentence when the first letter of each word is given. *Simple Interpretations* : Complete sentence that states an analogous idea.

Factor	Tests and Descriptions
	Word Arrangement ; Write sentences containing four specified words.
Ideational Fluency	*Topic If-1*: Write as many ideas as possible about given topic. (ETS). Theme If-2: Write as many words as possible about a given topic. (ETS) *Thing categories* If-3: List the names of "things that are round or that could be called round". *Ideational Fluancy* : Write names of things fitting into broad classes.
Semantic Spontaneous Flexibility	Brick Uses (flexibility): Write a variety of uses for a brick. *Alternative uses* : List different peculiar uses for common objects.
Associational Fluency	Controlled Associations : Write as many synonyms as possible for each given word. *Simile Insertions* : Write objectival completion for a simile. Associations IV : Produce a word that can be associated with two given words. *Associational Fluency* - 1: Write synonyms for given words.
Originality	*Plot titles* (clever) : Write clever titles for story plots. *Symbol Production* : Produce symbols to represent activities and objects. *Consequences* (remote) List remote consequences of certain changes.
Semantic Elaboration	Planning Elaboration : Fill in as many details as necessary to make briefly outlined activity or work. *Figure production* : Add to given lines to produce a meaningful figures. Score is based on number of details drawn.

Factor	*Tests and Descriptions*
Figural Redefinition (defining or perceiving in a way different from the usual established, or intended way, uses, etc.)	*Concealed figures CF-1* : Indicate which of four complex geometrical figures contains a given geometrical figure. (ETS) *Penetration of Camouflage* : Locate faces hidden in pictures. (USAP). *Hidden Pictures* : Find human or animal pictures hidden in a scene, as rapidly as possible. (Thurstone) *Hidden figures* : Indicate which of five figures is hidden in a given figure.
Symbolic Redefinition	*Camouflaged words* : Find the name of the sport or game sport or game concealed in a sentence. *Word Transformation* : Indicate new divisions between letters in a new varies of words forming a phrase, to make a new series of words.
Semantic Redefinition	*Gestalt Transformation* : Indicate which of five listed objects has a part that will serve a specified purpose. *Object synthesis* : Name on object that could be made by combining two specified objects.

THE ASSOCIATIVE CONCEPT OF CREATIVITY

Although the associative concept of creativity can be traced back to traditional associationism, the contemporary development here can be credited to Maltzman (1960) and Mednick (1962). Noticing that a word association test, with weighted scoring for statistical infrequencies of responses, can be a measure of individual differences in the factor of originality (Wilson at al. 1954). Maltzman and his collaborators (1958,1960) apply this criterion of originality (the formation of new combinations of associative elements) in a series of experiments on training for originality.

Similarly, taking clauses from the introspective reports of man's writings regarding their own creative functioning (as reported in Ghiseling (1952) for example), and defining creativity in associative terms as "the forming of associative elements into new combinations which either meet specified requirements or in some way useful : Mednick (1962) elaborates the theory of originality. He thinks that there are three ways of arriving at creative solution. He calls these serendipity, similarity and mediation. He supposes that in connection with each stimulus word each individuals has ahierachy of possible responses with more conventional and stereotyped associates higher in the hierarchy and more unique responses, lower. The stereotyped responses, he believes, are elicited more readily than the unique or uncommon ones, for the former, he thinks, possesses greater associative strength than the latter. Thus he assumes that the degree of the readiness of a particular response to be elicited can be expressed in terms of probability of occurrence. He believes that the probability gradient for the stereotyped responses has a sharp slope and hat the same for the unique responses a shallow slope. In other words, the gradient of a shallow slope is taken by him as representing a reprortorire containing a large number of congnitive elements, and that of a sharp slope as representing a repertoire containing a smaller number. Thus, this gradient contrast, according to Mednick, links high creative with a shallow slope and low creative with a sharp slope.

Based on this theory, Mednick (1962,1968) develops an assessment device, known as the Remote Association Test (RAT), for measuring creativity. In this, for each of the items, the subject has to provide a single word as an associative bridge to unite there given words. In each case only one word constitutes the correct answer. As a rule, this associative response is at a low operability in almost anybody hierachy. The criticisms advanced against this approach are many. First of all it is not known what factor or factors it measures, Secondly, it is concerned primarily with convergent thinking and does not attempt to cover the many divergent production and transformation abilities. Thirdly, it is very artificial in the sense that it tries to assess the creativity of the subjects on the basis of their tendency to choose the creative 'product' that has been predetermined for them.

Even while acknowledgeing the value of the time-honoured

associationism, one has to suspect its limited scope in the context of a theory of Creativity. Guilford (1967 b), for examples, states that ...to achieve an adequate theory (of creativity) it is necessary to go well beyond the association principle". He calls attention to the six psychological products of S I model and points out the advantages of having six varied concepts instead of a single concept of association. Thus he goes on to say:" If we attempt to get along with that single concept, we either apply it very loosely to a whole range of phenomena or we have to ignore many of them". Another difficulty with the associative interpretation of creative thinking is its assumption that nothing can be recalled in connection with another thing, unless the two are experienced (contiguously) in the past. This contention does not agree even with common sense. Thus contiguity, the corner stone of associationasim, fails pathetically in accounting for the bringing forth a new elements in creative production. The principle of association by similarity, although not much attended to by investigators, appears to be more promising here.

Creativity and Intelligence

Perhaps the most significant contribution of the last two decades of research on the structure of human abilities is the growing emphasis now given to creativity as a subject for empirical study. The two well known researchers of Guilford and his associates at the university of California on the structure of Intellect (1950,1956) have brought to the fore the existence of two distinct types of thinking abilities, namely, convergent thinking and divergent thinking, the former involving the generation of ideas and facts from known information, the later pertaining to new ideas or date which minimally depend on known information. In terms of the end results, convergent thinking implies a "singe already ascertained right response" whereas divergent thinking results in a "variety of responses involving fluency, flexibility, originality and elaboration". With the distinction thus made, convergent thinking came to be identified with intelligence as usually defined and measured by the well known intelligence tests, while divergent thinking gave the most obvious indication of what is generally understood by the term "creativity".

However, various analysis of the relationship between

scores on specific tests designed to measure creativity and those on tests designed to measure intelligence have failed to support such a sharp differentiation (Piers, Daniels & Quackenbush, 1960; Ripple and May 1962; Ricards, Cline & Needham, 1964; Klausmeier and Weirsma, 1965; Cropley, 1966).

Creativity, like intelligence is a many faced concept. Each term covers many abilities identified with relatively independent factors. Most available creativity tests were designed to measure different factors identified by Gilford within the broadly inclusive category of divergent production. One should not, therefore, except higher co-relations among scores on such tests than are found among scores on the different tests within the traditional area of intelligence, such as verbal comprehension and numberical reasoning tests.

The term's creativity' like the term 'intelligence' be recognised as referring to a loosely defined, broad, and many faceted concept. Both terms will undoubtedly serve as independent concept because they provide independent short cuts in designating complex behaviour, domains of considerable practical importance. But neither corresponds to precisely defined or distinct entity. Each comprises identifiable traits organised in a pattern of relationships that cut across the two domains (Anastasi and Schaefer, 1971).

A general factor of intellectual functioning involving measures of creativity and intelligence followed by two subseent factors of intelligence and creativity were obtained indicating that creativity and intelligence are two distinguishes modes of same intellectual functioning yet at the same time they are not disntictly independent of each other. This conclusion is akin to the concept of "cognitive style" (Within et al, 1954 : Ausbel and Ausbel, 1966). "modes of intellect" (Burt, 1962: Wallach and Kogan, 1965). 'Patterns of styles' (ardner, 1964); and 'intellectual bias' (Hudson, 1966).

A summary of researches on creativity and intelligence, conducted in this country and abroad, reveals that the relationship between the two is controversial, uncertain and of varying degree. From her factor analysis, Gulati (1982) affirms that creativity and intelligence constitutes distinct factors relatively independently of each other. Creativity, whether verbal or non-verbal asserts Gupta (1982), does not depend upon intelligence. Thus the relationship between creativity and intelligence is inconclusive and speculative. A detailed review of research findings regarding the co-relation between the two variables are presented under the section. What Research Surveys Convey' in chapter - IV.

Creativity in Relation to Culture

Introduction

The present chapter is devoted to survey of relation of culture (urban, rural, tribal) and creativity, Sex as related to creativity. This chapter also includes objectives, hypotheses, sample, tools used, statistical techniques applied in relation to culture and creativity.

Analysis and interpretation of results are made with reference to creativity and culture, sex difference in creativity in different cultural groups. This chapter also deals with the inter-groups sex-differences in creativity.

WHAT RESEARCH SURVEYS CONVEY

Culture as Related to Creative in Different Groups

A few studies were available on region as related to creativity which are quite inadequate to give a clear picture of rural, urban and tribal differences in creativity. Those studies are reviewed as under :

STUDIES REFLECTING "RURAL SUPERIORITY"

A number of studies (Torrance, 1960: Sharma, 1972 and 1974; Mehdi, 1973; Azmi, 1974) reported the superiority of rural children than their counterpart (urban children.). In a classical study involving several thousand children, Torrance (1960) found that in America there were differently more signs of tolerance of non-conformity in thinking among rural and town children than among urban children. The signs of creativity tolerance were observed in written stories. The percentage who tolerated nonconformity in writing stories (deviating conditions) in various groups were : urban 38, medim size own 68, and rural, 74. Sharma's (1972) study on urban-rural differences revealed that rural children were significantly more creative than their rural counterparts. Again Sharma (1974) studied 204 urban and 210 rural Xth class male students and concluded that rural subjects were more creative than their urban counterparts. In a workshop on "creativity through education" organised by the Regional College of Education, Bhopal, Mehdi (1973) mentioned that on both verbal and non-verbal tests rural children appeared to be doing better than their urban counterparts on fluency and flexibility tests, though in originality they (rural children) were poor. Azmi (1974) again confirmed the superiority of rural children by utilizing Mehdi's creativity tests.

STUDIES REFLECTING THE "SUPERIORITY OF URBAN CHILDREN"

A few studies (Singh 1980; Dharmagandan, 1981; Shukla, 1982) showed the superiority of urban children as against their rural counterparts. Singh (1980) studied the patterns of creativity between rural and urban children in relation to socio-economic status and he found that urban children were more creative than the rural children.

In verbal part of creativity test urban children scored significantly higher than rural children (Dharmagandan 1981) Contrary to Sharma's findings, Shukla (1982) a verbs that among rural school students there is comparatively low level of creativity as against the students of urban schools.

Interestingly Mishra (1986) found that unlike urban and rural disadvantaged children creativity differed significantly between advantaged and disadvantaged children in both rural and urban sub-cultures. Advantaged children scored more than disadvantaged. Further creativity scores of disadvantaged children in rural, urban and tribal subjects differed significantly. The rural group secured highest scores in verbal creativity subjects, tribals were the second highest and urban children secured the lowest scores. But in case of non-verbal creativity sub-tests, tribal secured the highest score, rural children secured second highest and urban disadvantaged children secured the lowest scores.

STUDIES REFLECTING "NO DIFFERENCE"

Along with the studies reflecting rural superiority and urban superiority, some studies are available which reflect no difference in creativity of urban, rural and tribal children. Insignificant rural, urban difference in creativity score within the disadvantaged children was found by Singh (1980). Earlier, Aaron *et al* (1969) found no significant difference between creativity scores of rural and urban boys. As against the urban superiority in creativity. Hussain and Subay (1975) reported that the tribals were equally creative as their urban counterparts.

Interestingly on a randomly selected sample of two hundred and thirty five representative Indian pupils from grade VII and VIII of middle school belonging to four cultural groups. i.e. urban, rural tribal and refugee Bengali located in Raipur and Rajnandgaon districts of M.P. Shukla and Sharma (1987) administered tests of scientific creativity developed by investigators for measuring fluency, flexibility and originality dimensions of scientific creativity of the pupils. The result revealed that the mean scientific creativity scores of Indian tribal pupils were found lowest on various dimensions of scientific creativity though there existed no significant difference between tribal and rural, tribal and refugee pupils on the flexibility and originality. Further it was found that rural pupils scored higher on fluency dimension than refugee Bengali pupils but there was no flexibility and original components of creativity. Conclusions : The picture, revealed by reviewing this section, is not convincing, clear and somewhat vague. Culture, being a signficant factor for promoting or inhibiting creative growth in children is not studied entirely taking different culture groups (urban, rural and tribal) into account. Most of the studies reviewed above related to a particular culture. Some studies, however, took a comparative culture of two. But none of the studies took urban, rural and tribal culture at a time in studying the creative potential of the students.

Sex as Related to creativity in Different Groups

Adequate understanding of the relationship between creativity and sex is necessary in developing methods of identifying and fostering creative thinking abilities of students. Over emphasis or misplaced emphasis on sex role, however, does exact its toll on the creativity of both the sexes and does create serious problems of adjustment for highly creative individuals of both the (Torrance, 1969). A resume of research findings about sex difference in creativity reveals different trends which are presented below under different headings.

STUDIES REFLECTING "SUPERIORITY OF MALES OVER FEMALES"

There are studies which support the superiority of male over the female students (Strauss and Strauss, 1968; Raina, 1971; Naintara, 1981; Dharmangandan, 1981). In a composite study of Indian and American children, Strauss and Strauss (1968) reported lower creativity of girls than those of boys. Sex difference in creativity were greatest in India. The smaller sex difference among American subjects is interpreted in terms of greatest freedom allowed to American girls. Similar to Strauss and Strauss Raina (1969, 1971) found that girls were less creative than boys. Study of Naintara (1981) reported that males excelled, as compared to females, on measures of verbal fluency, verbal flexibility, figural originality and figural elaboration. The contention that male students, in general, are more creative than female students was supported by the findings of Shukla and Dharmangendan also.

STUDIES REFLECTING SUPERIORITY OF FEMALES OVER MALES

Arriving at somewhat different and opposite conclusion the superiority of females over males in creativity score was also reported by MacGrego and Smith (1965) Harlow (1967) Ogletra (1971), Passi (1972, 1973), Harison (1973) and Hussain (1974). Studying the originality of elementary and high school students Mac Grego and Smith (1965) found girls to be more creative than boys. Such finding was also observed by Harlow (1967) using test of originality devised by Guildord. The girls also excelled than boys in verbal elaboration and some other measures of creative thinking (Torrance, 1962,1965); Torrance and Alicti, 1960), in fluency factors (Guilford, 1964 b) in verbal fluency (Dhir, 1973), Again the female superiority over male in measures of creativity was recorded and supported by Ogletre (1971), Passi (1973), and Harison (1973). Interestingly Hussain (1973) in his research found that the creativity scores of female group always acceded the male group but the difference was significant only n unusual tests. Going one step further Singh (1978) recorded that girls possess higher levels of word fluency, expressive fluency, spontaneous flexibility and originality than boys, but mainly in semantic content and in figural elaborating the two groups found same. On a sample of there hundred and twenty (101 males and 219 females) a adolescents randomly selected from the grade II population of 8 urban high schools administering five creativity tests (such as word association (Getzels and Jackson, 1962); unusual uses (Guilford and. Hoepthner, 1966): Fables (Getzels and Jackson, 1962); circles (Torrance, 1962); and Remote Association (Mednick, 1962) to the subjects in a relaxed class room atmosphere, without the pressure of time limit. Ricardson (1986) found significant difference infavour of the females beyond the .001 level. In addition to this there was large number of significant correlations between sex of the subjects and performance on the creativity measures was examined. Confirming the trends, female superiority over male in creativity, Stimpson (1986) observed boys to be less creative than girls.

Studies Reflecting "No Sex Difference"

With respect to fluency, flexibility and elaborating between the means of both male and female school children drawn from two different cities of two different states of India, Hussain and Hussain (1975) did not find significant sex differences. However, Badrinath and Satyanarayan (1979) mentioned that except in originality, there was no sex difference in respect of other components of creativity. On the same line Pandey and Pandey (1984) reported that there was no consistent sex difference in respect of various creativity factors (Though it was evident from his results that 10th grade female students mean creativity scores were significantly higher than 10th grade male students in elaboration). On a sample of 148 adolescents with the age group 15th from class IXth from six selected schools (one boys school, two girls schools and three co-educational schools) 74 (80%) boys and 74 (80%) girls was selected on the basis of proportionate random, sampling. Mehdi's creativity test both verbal and non-verbal was used. It was found that there was no difference in verbal creativity among the tribal boys and girls though, the non-verbal creativity of girls was higher than boys (Dutta, 1982).

Study Reflecting "Dual Trend"

Following the middle way Pandey (1981) reported that boys mean scores are better for fluency and flexibility than girls. Whereas girls mean scores are better for originality and composite creativity scores as compared to boys.

Conclusion

This critical review of researches on sex difference in creativity revealed that research findings about sex differences in creativity were varied. They ranged from cases where no discernible sex differences were observed, to situations where such differences were somewhat pronounced. Hence, the need to study the sex difference from different socio-cultural point is of prime importance.

Sample of the Study

The chief purpose of the present investigation was to study the creative potential of urban, rural and tribal adolescents of Western Orissa. The population of the study was Secondary school students (class IX) of Western Orissa. Two things have been taken into consideration by the investigator regarding the quality (representativeness) and quantity (total number) of the sample. The investigator selected four districts of Western Orissa namely, Sambalpur, Sundargarh, Bolangir and Kalahandi on the basis of major urban, rural and tribal concentration. The selection of the schools from above mentioned districts was purpose. Out of total twenty four schools, there were four boys schools and four girls schools (or urban area); eight coeducational and one girls school (or rural area); one boys school, four girls schools and two co-educational schools (of tribal area). The tribal sample was drawn from the schools run

Table 3.1
Break up of the Sample Selected for the Study

Sl. No.	*Name of the School*	*Area*	*District*	*Type of School School*	*No. of Boys*	*No. of Girls*	*Total*
1	*2*	*3*	*4*	*5*	*6*	*7*	*8*
1.	Municipality Girls High School Bargarh.	Urban	Samalpur	Girls	—	25	25
2.	Town High School, Bargarh	- do -	-do -	Boys	25	—	25
3.	Govt. Girls High School, Sundargarh	-do-	-do-	Boys	—	25	25
4.	B.S. High School, Sundargarh	-do-	-do-	Boys	25	—	25
5.	Govt. Girls High School, Titilagarh	-do-	Bolangir	Girls	—	25	25
6.	Mahesar Hindi High School,	-do-	-do-	Boys	25	—	25
7.	Govt. Girls High School, Bhawanipatna	-do-	Kalahandi	Girls	—	28	28
8.	B.M. High School, Bhawanipatna	-do-	-do-	Boys	25	—	25
9.	Gandhi M. High School, Kalapani	Rural	Sambapur	Co-education	14	11	25
10.	R.K.P. High School, Kumbharbangh	-do-	-do-	-do-	14	11	25
11.	Tilia High School, Tilia	-do-	-do-	-do-	05	11	16
12.	Lankahada High School, Lankahada	-do-	Sudargarh	-do-	15	09	24
13.	Bheda Bahal Girls School	-do-	-do-	Girls	—	24	24
14.	Pallisri High School, Sindhekela	-do-	Bolangir	Co-education	11	14	25
15.	Panchayat High School, Kholan	-do-	-do-	-do-	23	04	27
16.	Bijapur High School	-do-	-do-	-do-	15	07	22
17.	Kasrupada High School	Rural	Kalahandi	Co-Education	17	08	25

(Contd.)

	2	3	4	5	6	7	8
8.	Nrusinghanath TRW	Tribal	Sambalpur	-do-	—	03	25
9.	Kanyasram, Padampur	-do-	-do-	Girls	—	25	25
20.	Deokaranpur TRW	-do-	Sundargarh	Boys	25	—	25
21.	Tudalaga Girls High School, Tudalaga	-do-	-do-	Girls	—	24	24
22.	Saintala Kanyashram, Saintala	-do-	Bolangir	Girls	—	·25	25
23.	Chudapali TRW High School, Chudapali	-do-	-do-	Co-Education	25	01	26
24.	Junagarh Kanyashram, Junagarh.	-do-	Kalahandi	Girls	—	14	14
	Total				286	294	580

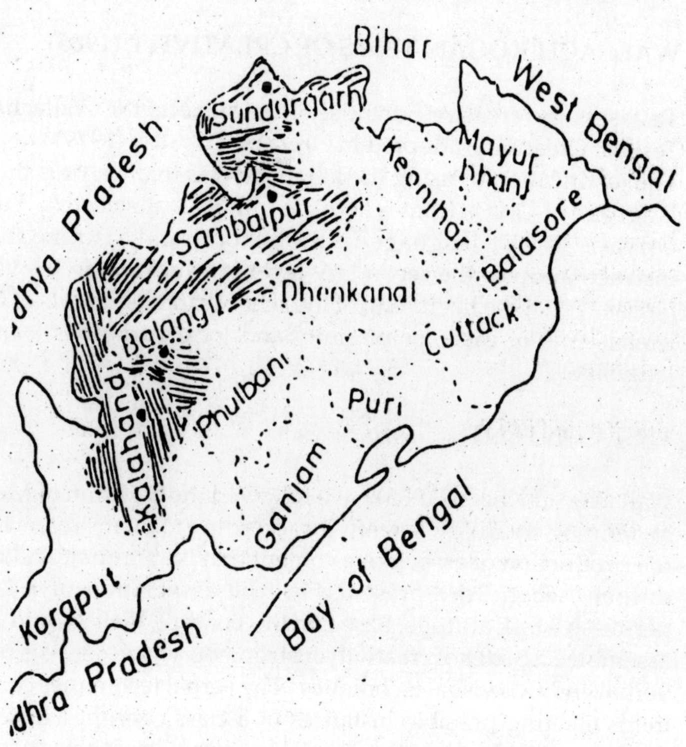

Fig. 3.1 Showing Area of Data Collection Orissa

under Tribal Rural Welfare scheme of (TRW), Govt. of Orissa. On the whole a total of 580 randomly drawn subjects of class IX from urban, rural and tribal areas (204 Ss urban, 213 Ss rural, and 163 Ss tribal) constituted the sample of the present investigation. A detailed picture of the total simple is presented in Table 3.1 and area of sample is located in Figure No. 3.1

INSTRUMENT USED

WALLACH KOGAN TESTS OF CREATIVITY (1965)

To assess the creative potential of the subjects the Wallach-Koan Tests of Creativity, adopted in Oriya by Tripathy (1979) was used. The justification of using the language was that Oriya is the local language of Orissa from where the sample was selected. Further, Oriya is the Ist language in the schools and also medium of instruction up to the secondary level of education in the state of Orissa. From the beginning of the school career students of Orissa irrespective of caste, community and local variations learn this language.

TEST CONTENT

Wallach and Kogan (1965) have followed the tradition of Mednick in defining creativity. Creativity according to them , refers to first, the production of associative content that is abundant and that is unique, second the presence in t he association of a lawful, permissive task attitude. Based on this concept, Wallach and Kogan assembled a better of creativity instruments which consists of three verbal and two visual techniques. The verbal techniques comprise items eliciting possible instances of a class concept (Instances), the items eliciting possible uses of a specified objects (Alternate uses), and items eliciting possible similarities between two verbally specified objects (Similarities). The two visual techniques consist of visual design (Pattern mean sings) and line drawings (line meanings). These serve as stimuli for the subject to generate possible meaning or interpretation. Short descriptions about each of the tasks is given below :

INSTANCES

This is the first of three verbal techniques. In this an individual is asked to generate possible instances of a concept that is specified in verbal terms. Example : Write all the round things you can think of.

ALTERNATE USES

In this, second of three verbal techniques, the individual is to write down the possible uses for a specified object. Example : write all the different ways you could use a newspaper.

SIMILARITIES

In the parents instrument the individuals is required to generate possible similarities between two specified objects. Examples : Write all the ways in which a potato and a carrot are alike.

PATTERN MEANINGS

This is one of the two creativity assessment techniques involving visual rather than verbal stimulus materials. It consists of eight items in addition to the example.

LINE MEANINIGS

This is the second creativity procedure involving stimulus materials. The individual is confronted with one another kind of line and is asked to generate meaning or interpretations relevant to the form of line in question. Line is a single continuous unit, in contrast to the discrete elements comprising the patterns in the preceding instruments.

TEST CONTENTS

The Wallach-Kogan tests of creativity have been found to be applicable to all age levels. For example, the tests have been used at Kindergarten level by Biller et al. Singe and Rummo (1973), at elementary level by Wallach and ogan (1965), and Rotter (1971) at the high school level by Applieton (1969) and at the University level by Cropley (1969), Cropley and Haslany (1969) and Wallach, Kogan and Wing (1969).

In India these tests were used by Paramesh (1969) in his doctoral thesis on University students. Wadhera (1974) used these tests on adolescents. Arun Gopal (1974) with due approval of the authors used these tests on adults in his doctoral thesis. Tripathy (1979) used the Oriya version of these tests, adopted and standardised by him, on school children. The same oriya version was also used by Mishra (1982) on schoolchildren and Sarangi (1984) on teacher pupils.

Various modes of administering these tests have been found by different investigators. Wallach and Kogan (1965) have used individual administration in their study, other modes of administration have also been adopted successfully by Cropley (1968) and Wallach and Wing (1969). The former investigator had administered the instruments in group from and the latter through mailing. In addition, the need for non-evaluative and stress free context for administration of creativity instruments has been recognised as important in a number of studies (Dentler & Mackler, 1964; Houston & Mednick, 1963; Mednick, Mednick and Jung, 1964; Wallach and Kogan, 1965; Wallach & Wing 1969). Since different methods of administration at different age level of these creativity instruments have been found to be valid, in the present study the investigator preferred to administer these tests in group form at high school stage.

RELIABILITY

Two approaches to reliability were taken by the authors of these instruments. The first was to calculate the split-half reliability of each measure according to the Spearman-Brown prophecy formula. They found substantial split-half reliability coefficients eight of the ten coefficients exceeded. 80. The measurers concerning number of associates for all the procedures - Instances, Alternate Uses, Similarities, Pattern meanings and Line Meanings-proposed a high degree of internal consistency. The split-half reliability of each of the creativity measures was ascertained by Wallach and Kogan (1965) on a sample of 151 children. The results are summarised in the Table 3.2 :

Cropley and Maslancy (1969) working on Indian sample of 100 adolescent boys found the Wallach-Kogan tests to be highly reliable and consistent. The coefficient of correlations are found by Spilt-half method by applying spearman-Brown formula. The reliability coefficients for each of instruments are given in the following table:

Table 3.2

Variable	*Reliability*	*Coefficient*
Instances	Uniqueness	.51
	Number	.75
Alternate Uses	Uniqueness	.87
	Number	.93
Similarities	Uniqueness	.87
	Number	.93
Pattern Meanings	Uniqueness	.88
	Number	.93
Line Meaning	Uniqueness	.82
	Number	.93

Table 3.3

Sub-tests	*No = 100*	*Obtained*	*Coefficient of 'r' by Spearman-Brown Formula*
Instances	Uniqueness	.40	.57
	Number	.56	.76
Alternate uses	Uniqueness	.56	.72
	Number	.22	.36
Similarities	Uniqueness	.61	.76
	Number	.72	.84
Pattern Meaning	Uniqueness	.70	.82
	Number	.83	.86
Line Meaning	Uniqueness	.72	.84
	Number	.75	.91

Reliability of the same instruments by administering it to an Indian population was also obtained by Paramesh (1972). The split-half correlations for the ten creativity measures indicated that the instruments employed here have high reliability. The lowest coefficient of correlation among those was .36; all the rest exceeded, .50; eight of the ten correlations were above .70. The item-sum correlations for the two procedures on the five instruments obtained were of very high order in this study of the 68 coefficients, 58 exceeded .50. Most of the coefficients were .60 or higher. This again reaffirms the high reliability of the creativity instruments employed here. The split-half reliability by using Spearman-Brown prophecy formula of Wallach- Kogan tests of creativity (Oriya version) was also found by Tripathy (1979). The reliability coefficients for each of the instruments are given below :

Table 3.4

For Creativity in Oriya	*Spearman - Brown Split half Reliability Coefficients*	
Instances	Uniqueness	.63
	Number	.87
Alternative uses	Uniqueness	.77
	Number	.78
Similarities	Uniqueness	.77
	Number	.87
Pattern Meaning	Uniqueness	.77
	Number	.84
Line Meaning	Uniqueness	.73
	Number	.90

Therefore, it was evident that the reliability coefficients of Wallach - Kogan Test of creativity are sufficiently high.

In their second approach to find out the reliability of the instruments the authors (Wallach & Kogan) carried out the item analysis for each instrument. Such an item analysis consisted of item-sum correlations in which the scores of each item is correlated with total. All of the 78 item-sum correlations were, .40 or better and 71 of the 78 were .60 better. No item in any measure was being unrepresentative of what the measure assessed as a whole.

In the Oriya version of Wallach-Kogan tests of creativity, from the inter correlation of the 18 variables 153 coefficient of correlations were obtained, out of 153 correlations, 80 coefficeint of correlations, were found to be significant at .01 level and 7 more found to be significant at .05 level of signficant. The average inter correlation among variables was found to be .32 which is signficant at .01 level. Thus it is concluded that all the eighteen variables of Wallach-Kogan tests of creativity in oriya version are measuring the different element of the same cognitive ability which results in their high positive inter correlations.

VALIDIY OF WALLACH-KOGAN TEST BATTERY DISCRIMINANT VALIDITY

The W-K creativity battery was designed specifically to exhibit a high degree of interrelatedness between the various sub-tests and to exhibit a low degree of relationship with I.Q. scores. On both these counts the battery rates will. The ten creativity indicates are strongly correlated. Of the 45 correlations, 43 are signficant bound the .05 level, 41 bound the .01 level. An item analysis to determine the extent to which it is contributing to the score provided by the sum of all items indicated that all item-sum correlations were .40 or better; 71 of 78 were .60 or better. In addition, the verbal and visual indices were also highly inter-correlated, though less highly than verbal or visual measures were within themselves. Thus, whatever the battery measures appears to be a fairly notary phenomenon. Another characteristic of the tests is that they do not correlate with intelligence measures and are relatively independent of each other. Studies of Paramesh and Cropley also certified the above facts with regard to correlations between creativity tests and I.Q. tests, it was found that correlations out of the hundred computed exceeded 23.

Tripathy (1979) found that the correlation between creativity scores (oriya version) and I.Q. scores is positive and low. The creativity scores of oriya version are differently related to scores on a test of general intelligence.

PREDICTIVE VALIDITY

As with any measure designed to assess creativity or creative potential, the usefulness of the Wallach-Kogan measures depend on its ability to predict creative performance in a non-test context. A study by Wallach and Wing (1969) is the first attempt to validate the Wallach and Kogan measures. The authors report significant differences between high and low SAT (Scholastic. Apt. test verbal and Mathematical) college students who have achieved in these areas. However, students with high indeational fluency scores were more likely to participate and make contributions in leadership, art writing and science although not in music, drama or social service than were students with low ideational fluency scores.

Indirect evidence, about the validity of these tests is also provided by Paramash (1972). Thus, the Wallach-Kogan Battery of creativity instruments is a satisfactory measure of creativity. It satisfies the criterion laid down by the associational concept of creativity and at the same time over comes the shortcomings attributed to other tests of creativity. Hence, the Wallach-Kogan creativity test possessed a high degree of predictive validity.

CONSTRUCT VALIDITY

Mc Kinney, James and Forman (1977) examine the construct validity of the Wallach-Kogan Tests of creativity. They analysed the factors through the inter correlation table of Wallach-Kogan tests of creativity. Primary Mental ability test and three subjects of Lowa Test of Basic skills, on a sample of 129 second grades using the principal component method. The factor of creativity (i.e.) verbal creativity and figural creativity were yielded, that were independent to those of intelligence and achievement measures. Such an evidence obtained was the construct validity of the Wallach-Kogan tests of creativity. Factor analysis of inter correlation of Wallach Kogan Tests of creativity and intelligence by Fee (1968) with multi group factor method reported that the second order factor clearly differentiated between creativity and intelligence although they themselves are slightly correlated.

Therefore, it reveals that Wallach-Kogan tests of Creativity possessed sufficient validity.

As the Wallach-Kogan Tests of creativity was found to be reliable, valid measure of creativity, further culture free and ago free test, it was finally decided by the investigator to administer it for the collection of required data for the present study.

APPLICABILITY

As the medium of instruction of the school students is oriya. It was thought quite good to give them oriya version of W.K. test of creativity for getting accurate data and maximum cooperation. Further as mentioned earlier under the heading rest context that it is quite applicable to all age level and it can be applicable to group as a whole with proper caution of motivation, time free, stress less situation.

CREATIVITY AND CULTURE

Creative potential seeks its maximum actualization within the environmental conditions and socio-cultural influences. Socio-cultural disadvantage retards the development of both verbal and non-verbal creativity. Human beings are both beneficiaries and victims of their culture. One definition of culture would be, as Huxley believes, a machine for making it possible for human beings to develop their potential. Obviously outside of an organised culture it is virtually impossible for even the most gifted human being to develop and actualize what lies latent within him, but here there is a paradox because culture is not only a machine for helping us to actualize potentialities, it is also a machine for preventing us from actualizing them. Hence, to study the creative potential from cultural stand point is not only necessary but also rewarding.

"A STUDY OF CREATIVE POTENTIAL OF URBAN RURAL AND TRIBAL ADOLESCENTS"

Definition of the Terms Used

A short description of the major terms used in the present study are given below in order to avoid ambiguity and the possibility of confusion.

Creative Potential

Creative potential in this study, will mean those operationally defined ability measured by Wallach-Kogan Tests of Creativity and expressed accordingly. This creative potential comprises subjects verbal and figural creativity. It is also termed as composite creativity.

Verbal Creativity

Verbal creativity of the subjects was determined by their obtained scores on three items of verbal techniques, such as, instances, alternate uses and similarities of Wallach-Kogan creativity test battery.

Figural Creativity

Figural creativity of the subjects was indicated by their obtained scores on two visual techniques such as, pattern meanings and line meanings. These serve as stimuli for the subjects to generate possible meaning and interpretation.

Urban Group

In the present study urban adolescents referred to those secondary school students (class IX) belonging to town area of four districts, namely Sambalppur, Sundargarh, Bolangir and Kalahandi of Western Orissa. Subjects were drawn mainly from Govt. Boys and Girls Secondary schools of the above mentioned districts.

Rural Group

Rural adolescents, in the present study, referred to those subjects belonging to the village area living away from the town culture and atmosphere of Sambalpur, Sundargarh, Bolangir and Kalahandi districts, Most of the rural schools were private ones, a few were government aided. Almost all the rural schools were co-educational with only one exception which was a Girls school.

Tribal Group

The tribal adolescents in the present study referred to those randomly selected subjects who were admitted to secondary schools run by Tribal Rural Welfare Deptt. (TRW) Govt. of Orissa. Out of the total TRW schools majority were located in village area, one schools located in jungle area and a few in town area and town culture.

OBJECTIVES

The objectives of the present study are as follows :

1. To study the creative potentiality of Urban, Rural and Tribal adolescents.
2. To study the differences in verbal and non-verbal creativity in urban, rural and tribal adolescents.
3. To study the sex difference in creativity of urban, rural and tribal adolescents.

HYPOTHESIS

The hypotheses of the present study are as follows :

H_1 - There is no significant difference in creative potential in urban, rural and tribal adolescents.

H_2 - There is no significant difference in verbal and non-verbal creativity so far as urban, rural and tribal adolescents are concerned.

H_3 - There is no significant six difference in creativity among urban, rural and tribal adolescents.

METHODOLOGY AND PROCEDURE

Sample

On the whole a total of 580 randomly drawn subjects of class IX from urban, rural and tribal (204Ss urban, 213 Ss rural and 163 Ss tribal) constituted the sample of the present investigation. A detailed picture of the selection of the sample is presented earlier in this chapter in Table No. 3.1 and area of sample is located in Figure No. 3.1.

Instrument Used

To assess the creative potential of the subjects the allach-Kogan Tests of creativity adopted in Oriya by Tripathy (1979) was used. The justification of using this test and description of the test is presented in this chapter earlier.

Data Collection

The data for the present research work were collected by the investigator personally from schools of all the four selected districts of Western Orissa. Tests of Creativity were administered as per the procedure laid down in test manual.

Statistical Techniques Employed

In the present study several statistical techniques were employed to analyse the collected data for major study. According to the nature and complexity of the study, to test various hypotheses based on objectives of the study, different statistical treatment was needed.

i) Descriptive analysis : Means, SD's, 't' ratio and testing the significant difference between means were workout to compare the groups urban rural and tribal on creativity.

RESULTS AND DISCUSSION

Composite Creativity and Cultural Groups

In order to study the creative potential of students belonging to different cultural groups, means and standard deviations of composite creativity (verbal + figural) scores obtained on total urban, rural and tribal students were calculated separately. The results are given in Table 3.1

It is clear from Table 3.1 that meacreativity scores of urban adolescents is significantly higher than that of rural adolescents. The obtained 't' ration 4.09 is significant (P< .01). It indicates that there exists marked differences in creative potential of urban and rural adolescents and that urban adolescents, in general, are more creative than their rural counterparts.

The superiority of urban adolescents over their rural counterparts on creativity measures may be explained on the basis of various reasons; it may be due to the chances of greater opportunities and possibilities open to urban adolescents and their field independence in comparison to their rural counterparts. On the same line Tharakan (1987) reported that subjects who reside in urban environment will be relatively field independent than those in rural environment. This field independent cognitie style well suited to a culture those way of life seeks to achieve physical, material objectives in informal ways. It may also due to better social surrounding (Open society away from rigid traditional values). Earlier, the preponderance of urban over rural counterparts on creativity was also evidenced in Singh's (1980) findings.

Dharmangandan (1981) also found urban adolescents to be more creative than rural adolescents, while studying the population from secondary school children of Kerala using Torrance test of Creative thinking (TTCT).

Again, from the same table it is observed that between the mean composite creativity scores of rural and tribal adolescents the mean composite creativity scores of tribal adolescents is greater than rural adolescents and the 't' ration 1.97 is significant (P < .05). It may be concluded from the table that the tribal adolescents,

Table 3.1.1
Mean, Standard Deviation and t Values for Composite Creativity Scores of Total Urban, Rural and Tribal Groups

Groups	*N*	*Mean*	*SD*	't'
Urban	204	89.86	30.31	4.09 **
Rural	213	78.68	25.01	
Rural	213	78.68	25.01	1.97 *
Tribal	163	84.07	27.23	
Urban	204	89.86	30.31	1.92 N.S.
Tribal	163	84.07	27.23	

* Significant at .05 level

** Significant at .01 level

in general, are more creative than their rural counterparts. This may be due to the factor that tribal children are more natural, less pressurised by courteous behaviour and rules as compared to rural children. But it needs further confirmation through the data based on wider sample.

However, so far as the mean creativity scores of urban and tribal adolescents are concerned, urban adolescents scored higher than the tribal but the differences are not significant. Though many more studies are required to conclude finally the non-significant differences between urban and tribal adolescents. But for the present study various statistical and other inherent factors and reasons including achievement need might be responsible for gaining non-significant differences. Before long, Hussain and Subay (1975) had also found similar results and asserted that tribals are equally creative as their urban counterparts.

Thus, the first hypothesis of no difference is partially accepted. Urban and Rural groups, Rural and tribal groups differ significantly from one another, on creative potential. In the first two comparable groups urban group tribal group proves to be more creative. Only urban and tribal groups do not differ significantly which proves that tribals are equally creative as their urban counterparts on creative potential.

VERBAL/FIGURAL CREATIVITY AND CULTURAL GROUPS

Like composite creativity urban, rural and tribal subjects were compared on verbal and figural creativity to examine the data pertaining to hypothesis 2. Mean scores and standard deviations of verbal and figural creativity obtained on total urban, rural and tribal subjects were calculated separately and the results are presented in Tables 3.1.2 and 3.1.3 for verbal and figural creativity respectively.

From Tables Nos. 3.1.2 and 3.1.2 it is clear that while comparing the mean verbal and figural creativity scores of urban and rural adolescents, urban adolescents are more creative. On verbal creativity of urban and rural adolescents and obtained 't' ratio 3.93 is highly signficant ($P < .01$). Likewise on figural creativity of urban and rural subjects the obtained 't' ratio 3.86 is also highly significant ($P < .01$). This shows that urban

Table 3.1.2
Mean, Standard Deviation and 't' values for Verbal Creativity scores of total Urban, Rural and Tribal Groups

Groups	*N*	*Mean*	*SD*	*'t'*
Urban	204	53.76	16.83	3.93 **
Rural	213	47.64	14.94	
Rural	213	47.64	14.94	1.47 NS
Tribal	163	50.10	16.82	
Urban	204	53.76	16.83	2.07*
Tribal	163	50.10	16.82	

* Significant at .05 level

** Significant at .01 level

Table 3.1.3

Mean, Standard Deviation and 't' values for Figural creativity scores of total Urban, Rural and Tribal Groups

Groups	*N*	*Mean*	*SD*	't'
Urban	204	37.24	16.89	3.86 **
Rural	213	31.40	13.76	
Rural	213	31.40	13.76	1.24 NS
Tribal	163	33.27	15.00	
Urban	204	37.24	16.89	2.37*
Tribal	163	33.27	15.00	

* Significant at .05 level

** Significant at .01 level

subjects, in general, are more creative than their rural counterparts in respect of both verbal and figural creativity. This may be due to the fact that urban adolescents are exposed to great freedom in the form of thinking and expression and greater encouragement, less exposed to moral, social and family rules (unlike rural). The rural atmosphere limits children's imagination by social conservative values and expectations. Era long, Sing (1980) studied the pattern of creativity between rural and urban children in relation to socio-economic status and found that urban children were more creative than the rural children. In another study on a sample of secondary school children using Torrance Test of Creative Thinking (TTCT) Dharmangandan (1981) had found similar results and recorded that in verbal part of creativity test urban children scored significantly higher than the rural children. Shukla (1982) had also found that among rural school students, there was comparatively low creativity as against urban school students.

Further the same tables show somewhat lesser and insignificant mean score differences between the rural and tribal adolescents in respect of verbal and figural creativity. The difference in mean scores may be attributed to chance factor. Under the condition of present study significant differences between rural and tribal subjects on verbal and figural creativity was not found by the investigator.

Again, between the urban and tribal groups it was found that the mean verbal and figural creativity scores of urban subjects are significantly higher than that of tribal subjects. The obtained 't' rations 2.07 and 2.37 for verbal and figural creativity respectively are signficant ($P < .05$). Hence, the hypothesis of 'no difference' can be rejected so far as the urban and tribal groups on verbal and figural creativity are concerned. This shows that in verbal and figural creativity urban adolescents, in general, are more creative than their tribal counterparts. This may be due to socio-cultural variables including child rearing practices of parents, parent-child relationship. Greater awareness and possibilities for adolescents of urban background than the rural one. But it requires further validation through the data based on wider sample and different creativity measures.

Table 3.2.1

Mean, Standard Deviation and 't' Values For Urban Boys and Girls on Verbal, Figural and Composite Creativity

	Verbal		*Figural*		*Composite*	
	B	G	B	G	B	G
N	100	104	100	104	100	104
Mean	49.20	58.06	29.55	44.50	79.90	102.40
S.D.	18.03	19.09	12.90	16.27	29.80	26.40
't'	3.90**		4.88 **		5.70**	

* Significant at .05 level

** Significant at .01 level

SEX DIFFERENCES IN CREATIVITY IN DIFFERENT CULTURAL GROUPS

In the analysis of data pertaining to hypothesis 3, the means, standard deviations of total boys and girls of urban, rural and tribal adolescents were computed separately. Table Nos. 3.2.1, 3.2.2 and 3.2.3 showing the mean differences in verbal, figural and composite creativity of to all urban, rural and tribal adolescents were presented in relation to sex.

From Table 3.2.1 it is clear that the obtained mean scores of urban girls exceeds the obtained mean scores of urban boys in all the three components (viz. verbal, figural and composite) of creativity. And those differences are quite signficant. The obtained 't' rations 3.90 ,4.88 and 5.70 for verbal, figural and composite creativity of urban boys and girls are significant. In all the cases girls are superior to boys. It indicates that there exists a pronounced sex difference, favouring girls, in urban sub-culture. In verbal, figural and composite creativity girls mean scores are greater then those of boys. It means that urban girls are more creative than urban boys in all the components of creativity. The notability of girls over the boys in all the components of creativity may be explained from psycho-socio-cultrual perspective (such as greater autonomy for girls open and democratic environment, less exposed to traditionality, parental child rearing practices in urban culture. Earlier, similar findings on somewhat different culture was reported by Suess (1981). He found that Eskimo girls had higher scores on all the sub-tests of creativity than Eskimo boys and concluded that town environment was congenial for the development of creativity (in Eskimo) than village or city environment. Previously, many researchers found the similar trend in creativity potential. On a sample of three hundred twenty (101 males and 219 females) adolescents randomly selected from grade 11 population of 8 urban high schools administering creativity tests (such as, word association (Getzels and Jackson, 1962): Unusual uses (Guilford and Hoetner, 1966); Fables (Gatzels and Jackson, 1962); Circles (Torrance, 1962); and remote association (Mednick, 1982) to the subjects in a relaxed class room atmosphere, without the pressure of time limit, Richardosn (1986) found significant deference in favour of the females beyond the .001 level. In addition to this there was large number of signficant correlations

Table 3.2.2
Mean, Standard Deviation and 't' Values For Rural Boys and Girls on Verbal, Figural and Composite Creativity

	Verbal		*Figural*		*Composite*	
	B	G	B	G	B	G
N	114	99	114	99	114	99
Mean	51.08	43.12	34.94	31.54	85.70	69.57
S.D.	14.09	13.52	12.19	11.86	24.13	21.11
't'	4.21**		1.65 NS		5.20 **	

** Significant at .01 level

relating to females when the relationship sex of the subjects and performances on the creativity measures was examined. Confirming the trend, female superiority over the male in creativity Simpson (1986) observed buys to be less creative than girls.

From the Table 3.2.2 it is observed that the obtained mean scores of rural boys exceeds significantly from the obtained mean scores of rural girls on two the three components (viz verbal and Composite). The obtained 't' rations in verbal and composite creativity 4.21 and 5.20 respectively, are highly significant (P. 01). This indicates that there exist marked sex differences, favouring boys in rural sub-culture. In other words, it can be said that in verbal and composite creativity rural boys are more creative than rural girls. But in figural creativity, as the table suggests, sex difference is not a notable one and whatever a little difference exists can be attributed to chance factor. The superiority of rural boys over the girls in verbal and composite creativity can be explained again in terms of psycholocio-culture context. It may be due to freedom of expression and action that the boys enjoy in rural culture. Another reason may be that the socio expectation of roe playing of rural girls to be more submissive, obedient, conservative of social and moral rules as the indicators of good feminine virtue which impede the creative expression and performance of rural girls particularly in Oriya culture. Early, in a comosie study on Indian and American cultures strause and Strauss (1968) reported lower creativity of girls than those of boys both in America and India. In that it was found that sex differences were greatest in India. The smaller sex differences among the American subjects was interpreted in terms of freedom allowed to American girls. Again, raina (1969, 1971) found girls to be less creative than boys. Naintara (1981) found that males exccelled as compared to female on measures of verbal fluency, verbal flexibility, figural originality and figural elaboration. The turn of male superiority over the female was also evidenced from the studied of Dharmagandan (1981) and shukla (1982).

Analysis of the Table 3.2.3 indicates that the obtained mean scores of tribal boys exceeds the obtained mean scores of tribal girls in two of the three components of creativity (namely, figural and composite) significantly. The obtained 't' rations 4.46 and 2.18 in figural and composite creativity respectively are significant (P. 01 in figural and $P < .05$ in composite). It reveals that in figural and composite creativity tribal boys are superior to tribal girls.

Table 3.2.3
Mean, Standard Deviation and 't' Values For Tribal Boys and Girls on Verbal, Figural and Composite Creativity

	Verbal		*Figural*		*Composite*	
	B	G	B	G	B	G
N	72	91	72	91	72	91
Mean	49.08	51.53	39.63	29.72	89.92	80.60
S.D.	18.78	15.30	14.48	13.42	28.57	25.19
't'	.89NS		4.98 **		2.18 *	

* Significant at .05 level

** Significant at .01 level

But it is only on verbal creativity the two sexes do not differ significantly. Whatever a little deference that arises may be attributed t chance factor. The significant sex difference in figural and composite creating of tribal boys and girls, favouring boys may be explained in terms of socio-cultural factors. Though many more studies are required to conclude finally the significant differences between tribal boys and girls on figural and composite creativity. But for the present study various statistical and other inherent factors and reasons might be responsible for gaining non-significant differences in verbal creativity of tribal boys and girls. With regard to non-significant sex difference between tribal boys and girls only one study (Dutta, 1982) was reported that there was no difference in verbal creativity among the tribal boys and girls (though another finding of Dutta's study (1982) reported that non-verbal creativity of girls are higher than that of boys.

INTERGROUP SEX DIFFERENCES IN CREATIVITY

To extend the scope of sex difference in creativity in different cultural groups and to arrive at a clear, convincing and an adequate picture the investigator went beyond this in analysing the Inter-group sex difference in verbal, figural and composite creativity and examined 34 pairs (comparable groups).

Table 3.2.2.1 shows that between urban and rural groups in composite creativity only three pairs namely, urban boys and rural girls, urban girls and rural boys, urban girls and rural girls, did show significant differences favouring urban boys, urban girls and urban girls in above pairs respectively. The obtained 't' ratios 2.82,4.86 and 9.80 for the respective groups are highly significant ($P < .01$). The marked differences between the group urban boys and rural girls, urban girls and rural boys, urban girls and rural girls may be due to various reasons. The table overvalues that urban boys are superior to rural girls which may be due to open environment and wide possibilities before urban boys. The combined relationship of sex and urbanisation was more predictive of field independence when urban males were compared with rural females (Tharaken, 1987). The findings of Tharakan's study support Within's differentiation hypotheses that field independence depend with perceptual cognitive aea related to a more general syndrome. Another possible reason may be the more filed independence in case of urban boys than rural girls. The

Table 3.2.2.1

Inter-group Gender Differences in Composite (Total) Creativity of Urban and Rural Groups

Groups	*N*	*Mean*	*SD*	*'t'*
Urban Boys	100	79.90	29.80	1.55 N.S.
Rural Boys	114	85.70	24.13	
Urban Boys	100	79.90	29.80	2.82 **
Rural Boys	99	69.57	21.11	
Urban Boys	104	102.40	26.40	4.86 **
Rural Boys	114	85.70	24.13	
Urban Boys	104	102.40	26.40	9.80**
Rural Boys	99	69.57	21.11	

** Significant at .01 level

table also reveals that urban boys than rural girls. The table also reveals that urban girls are superior to rural boys. It may be owing to better material and psychological freedom to act and think independently in case of urban girls than rural boys. Urban girls are superior to rural girls was evident from the table also may be due to greater freedom enjoyed by urban girls than the rural girls. Whatever a little insignificant differences that exist between urban boys and rural boys may be attributed to chance.

Table 3.2.2.2 indicates between rural and tribal groups only two pairs namely rural girls and tribal boys (favouring tribal girls) were found to be highly significant. The obtained 't' rations 5.11 and 3.26 for respective groups are highly signficant (P <.01). The table does not indicate any such marked differences in pairs like rural boys and tribal boys, and rural boys and tribal girls. Whatever a little difference that exist may be due to chance factor. The superiority of tribal boys over rural girls and tribal girls and tribal girls over rural girls may be explained in terms of their achievement need inherent in their culture. High achievement need is a prerequisite for creative performance which is even evidenced by this present investigator and will be discussed in this present investigator and will be discussed in this chapter. In developing the theory of achievement motive Mehta (1974) explained the high achievement need in tribal people in terms of their realization of their status of backwardness which is responsible in promoting greater achievement need in them. And what the present investigator assumes it is that motive to achieve through which they showed superior creativity over the rural subjects in composite creativity.

Table 3.2.2.3 indicates that between urban and tribal groups 3 pairs out of four, namely, urban boys and tribal boys, urban girls and tribal boys, urban girls and tribal girls were found significantly different in their mean composite creativity scores. The obtained 't' rations 2.23,.2.94 and 5.89 for respective pairs are found to be significant (P< .05 for the first pair, and P< 01 for the second and third pairs). It is clear from the table 6.1.. 6.3 that in first pair, between urban boys and tribal boys, tribal boys superseded urban boys. Between urban girls and tribal boys, urban girls exceeded tribal boys. And between the urban girls and tribal girls urban girls exceeded tribal girls. In the first pair, the superiority of tribal boys over urban boys may be explained in terms of greater need

Table 3.2.2.2

Inter-group Gender Differences in Composite (Total) Creativity of Rural and Tribal Groups

Groups	*N*	*Mean*	*SD*	*'t'*
Rural Boys	114	85.70	24.13	1.04 N.S.
Tribal Boys	72	89.92	28.57	
Rural Boys	114	85.70	24.13	1.47 N.S.
Tribal Girls	91	80.60	25.20	
Rural Girls	99	69.57	21.11	5.11**
Tribal Boys	72	89.92	28.57	
Rural Girls	99	69.57	21.11	3.26**
Tribal Boys	91	80.60	25.20	

** Significant at .01 level

Table 3.2.2.3

Inter-group Gender Differences in Composite (Total) Creativity of Urban and Tribal Groups

Groups	*N*	*Mean*	*SD*	't'
Urban Boys	100	79.90	29.80	2.23*
Tribal Boys	72	89.92	28.57	
Urban Boys	100	79.90	29.80	.17 N.S.
Tribal Boys	91	80.60	25.20	
Urban Boys	104	102.40	26.40	2.94 **
Tribal Boys	72	89.92	28.57	
Urban Boys	104	102.40	26.40	5.89**
Tribal Boys	91	80.60	25.20	

* Significant at .05 level

** Significant at .01 level

achievement in tribal boys. Earlier, Mehta (1974) while theorizing the achievement motivation reported tribals having greater achievement need because of their realizaiton of backwardness. The notability of urban girls over tribal boys and tribal girls in second and third significant pairs respectively on composite creativity may be due to greater freedom, opportunities and urbanization inherent in urban culture. A negligible mean different that exists between the pair - urban boys and tirbal girls may be attributed to chance factor.

Table 3.2.2.4 indicates that between the urban and rural groups on verbal creativity, three pairs out of four differed significantly. The obtained 't' ratio 2.69,7.71 and 3.65 in case of urban boys and rural girls (favouring urban boys), urban girls and rural girls (favouring urban girls) and urban girls and rural boys (favouring urban girls) respectively are highly significant (P<.01). In all the significant pairs between urban and rural groups urban adolescents of either sex proved themselves superior in verbal creativity. The superiority of urban adolescents, in general, over their rural counterparts especially on verbal creativity may be unreported and explained in terms of socio-cultural values. Urban girls in general, enjoy greater freedom and safety then their rural counterparts, Psychological safety and freedom as Meslow (1956) believes, foster individuals creativity, Between the urban and rural groups only open pair newly, urban boys and rural boys did not differ significantly. Whatever a little difference that exist may be attributed to chance factor.

Table 3.2.2.5 revels that between the rural and tribal groups on verbal creativity significant differences were only found in such airs like, rural girls and tribal boys, rural girls and tribal girls. As the table shows the first and second pairs such as rural boys and tribal boys rural boys tribal girls did not differ significantly in their mean verbal creativity scores. Whatever a little difference exists may be attributed to chance factor. However, in the same table the 't' ration of the third and fourth airs 2.29 and 4.004 are significant (P< .05 and P. 01 respectively). It shows that in verbal creativity tribal boys are more creative than rural girls. This may be due to their higher achievement motivation. Again, it is clear from the table that tribal girls are more creative than rural girls. This may also be explained on the similar ground, however, many more studies based on wider sample are required to confirm the findings of the present study.

Table 3.2.2.4
Inter-group Gender Differences in Composite (Total) Creativity of Urban and Rural Groups

Groups	*N*	*Mean*	*SD*	*'t'*
Urban Boys	100	49.20	18.03	.84 N.S.
Rural Boys	114	51.08	14.09	
Urban Boys	100	49.20	18.03	2.69 **
Rural Boys	99	43.12	13.52	
Urban Boys	104	58.06	14.09	7.71 **
Rural Boys	99	43.12	13.52	
Urban Boys	104	58.06	14.09	3.65**
Rural Boys	114	51.08	14.09	

** Significant at .01 level

Table 3.2.2.5

Inter-group Gender Differences in Composite (Total) Creativity of Urban and Tribal Groups

Groups	*N*	*Mean*	*SD*	't'
Rural Boys	114	51.08	14.09	.77 N.S.
Tribal Boys	72	49.08	18.78	
Rural Boys	114	51.08	14.09	.21 N.S.
Tribal Boys	91	51.53	15.30	
Rural Boys	99	43.12	13.52	2.29 *
Tribal Boys	72	49.08	18.78	
Rural Boys	99	43.12	13.52	4.004 **
Tribal Boys	91	51.53	15.30	

* Significant at .05 level

** Significant at .01 level

Table 3.2.2.6
Inter-group Gender Differences in Verbal Creativity of Urban and Tribal Groups

Groups	*N*	*Mean*	*SD*	*'t'*
Urban Boys	100	49.20	18.03	.14 N.S.
Tribal Boys	72	49.08	18.78	
Urban Boys	100	49.20	18.03	.96 N.S.
Tribal Boys	91	51.53	15.30	
Urban Boys	104	58.06	14.09	3.08 **
Tribal Boys	91	51.53	15.30	
Urban Boys	104	58.06	14.09	3.44 **
Tribal Boys	72	49.08	18.78	

** Significant at .01 level

Table 3.2.2.6 indicates that between urban and tribal groups on verbal creativity the first two pairs namely urban boys and tribal girls did not show any marked difference in their mean creativity scores. Whatever a little difference exists may be due to chance factor. But in 3rd and 4th pairs namely, urban girls and tribal girls, urban girls and tribal boys differed significantly in their mean creativity scores especially on verbal creativity. The obtained 't' ration 3.08 between urban girls and tribal girls and 3.44 between urban girls and tribal boys are significant (P < .01). Between urban girls and tribal girls, urban girls superseded tribal girls. This means that no verbal creativity urban girls, in general were more creative than tribal girls. So also in the next pair between urban girls and tribal boys, urban girls were more creative than tribal boys on verbal creativity. The superiority of urban girls over tribal girls and tribal boys may be due to socio-cultural and economic factors. However, many more studies are required to validate the findings of the present study.

It was observed from Table 3.2.2.7 that between urban and rural groups on figural creativity out of total four pairs signficant differences were found in three pairs such as, urban boys and rural boys, urban girls and rural boys, urban boys and rural boys, urban girls and rural boys, urab girls and rural girls. The obtained 't' rations 3.1.3, 4.87 and 6.51 between urban boys and rural boys, urban girls and rural boys, urban girls and rural girls respectively are signficant (P< .01). It reveals that between urban boys and rural boys, rural boys were found to be more creative, between urban girls and rural boys, urban girls were found to be more creative, and between urban girls and rural girls, urban girls were found to be more creative so far as figural creativity was concerned. The superiority of rural boys over urban boys ay be due to virus statistical and other inherent reasons and factors. Many more studies are required to confirm the findings of the study. Again, the notability of urban girls over rural girls on fairly creativity may be due to freedom enjoyed by urban girls in urban culture and atmosphere and their field independence. Tharaken (1987) asserted that subjects who reside in urban environment will be relatively more field independent then those in rural environment. Only one pair out of four namely, urban boys and rural girls did not show any marked difference on figural creativity. The insignificant difference may be due to chance factor.

Table 3.2.2.7
Inter-group Gender Differences in Verbal Creativity of Urban and Rural Groups

Groups	*N*	*Mean*	*SD*	't'
Urban Boys	100	29.55	12.90	3.13 **
Rural Boys	114	34.94	12.19	
Urban Boys	100	29.55	12.90	.34 N.S.
Rural Boys	99	31.55	11.87	
Urban Boys	104	44.50	16.27	4.87**
Rural Boys	114	34.94	12.19	
Urban Boys	104	44.50	16.27	6.51 **
Rural Boys	99	31.55	11.87	

** Significant at .01 level

Table 3.2.2.8
Inter-group Gender Differences in Figural Creativity of Rural and Tribal Groups

Groups	*N*	*Mean*	*SD*	't'
Rural Boys	114	34.94	12.19	2.29 *
Tribal Boys	72	39.64	14.48	
Rural Boys	114	34.94	12.19	5.65 **
Tribal Boys	91	29.72	13.42	
Rural Boys	99	31.55	11.87	.99 N.S.
Tribal Boys	91	29.72	13.42	
Rural Boys	99	31.55	11.87	3.889**
Tribal Boys	72	39.64	14.49	

* Significant at .05 level

** Significant at .01 level

Table 3.2.2.9
Inter-group Gender Differences in Figural Creativity of Urban and Tribal Groups

Groups	*N*	*Mean*	*SD*	't'
Urban Boys	100	29.55	12.90	4.71 **
Tribal Boys	72	39.64	14.48	
Urban Boys	100	29.55	12.90	.09 N.S.
Tribal Boys	91	29.72	13.42	
Urban Boys	104	44.50	16.27	2.08 *
Tribal Boys	72	39.64	14.49	
Urban Boys	104	44.50	16.27	6.94 **
Tribal Boys	91	29.72	13.42	

* Significant at .05 level

** Significant at .01 level

Table 3.2.2.8 indicates that between rural and tribal groups out of four pairs significant differences in mean figural creativity sources were found between rural boys and tribal boys, rural boys and tribal girls, rural girls and tribal boys. The obtained 't' ratios 2.29, 5.65 and 3.89 are significant (P< .05) for the first pair and P< .01 of the next two pairs). It means between rural boys and tribal boys tribal boys were found to be more creative especially on figural creativity. This may be due to greater achievement need possessed by tribal boys. Earlier, Mehta (1974) asserted that tribals are having found more achievement oriented because of the realization of their backwardness. Likewise between rural girls and tribal boys, tribal boys were more creative than rural girls and this may be due to the same reason described just before. However, between rural boys and tribal girls, rural boys were found to be more creative than tribal girls. This may be due to greater freedom opened to rural boys were found to be more creative than tribal girls. This may be due to greater freedom opened to rural boys than tribal girls. Many more studies are required on wider sample and using different measures of figural creativity to validate the findings of the present study. Whatever negligible difference that exists between the mean figural creativity scores between tribal girls and rural girls may be attributed to chance.

Table 3.2.2.9 indicates that between urban and tribal groups on figural creativity significant differences were found between three pairs such as urban, boys and tribal boys (favouring tribal boys), urban girls and tribal boys (favouring urban) girls and ribali girls (favouring urban girls). the obtained 't' rations 4.71, 2.08 and 6.94 are signficant (P< .01) P< .05 P< .01 respectively. Between urban boys and tribal boys tribal boys were more creative. It may be due to greater need achievement as explained earlier. However, many more studies are required to confirm the findings of the present study. Between urban girls and tribal girls, urban girls were more creative. Likewise between urban girls and tribal boys. Urban girls were more creative on figural creativity. This may be due to greater freedom opened to urban girls. Whatever a little differences that exists between the mean creativity scores of urban boys and tribal girls may be due to chance factors.

Creativity in Relation to Certain Variables

INTRODUCTION

The present chapter is devoted to meaning and concept of Achievement Motivation, Self-concept, and intelligence; Survey of related studies in relation to creativity and Achievement Motivation, Creativity and self-concept, and Creativity and Intelligence.

Brief description of the nature, content of measures of creativity, Achievement Motivation and Self-concept and Intelligence are also presented in this chapter.

This chapter also includes the detailed studies of creativity in relation to those above mentioned variables. Analysis and interpretation of results are made with reference to creativity and those variables such as achievement motivation, self-concept and intelligence.

CONCEPT OF ACHIEVEMENT MOTIVATION

In the area of motivation, much experimentation has been done on need achievement or achievement motivation which is currently a living topic of investigation. The first systematic approach to develop the concept of achievement motivation was initiated by David Mcclelland and his associates. They have produced a wealth of research on achievement motivation, Mcclelland argued that the achievement motivation, like other forms of human motivation, can best be studied in the realm of fantasy. Fantasy is fire in the sense that conditions of testing do not place external constraints on the responses that are possible. In a summary of his investigation on achievement motive Mcclelland at all write, "In general people with a high achievement imagery index score complete more tasks under achievement orientation, solve more simple arithmetic problems, in a timed test improve faster in their ability to do anagrams, tend to get better grades, use more future tense and abstract nouns in talking about themselves, set higher level of aspiration if reality factors are ruled out and to recall more incomplete tasks, score higher in interest maturity scale of Strong Vocational Interest Test, show a slight tendency recognise achievement related words faster and soon".

Achievement motivation is thus a learned motive complete and to strive for success. Because almost any activity from gardening to managing an industrial organization can be viewed in terms of competition and success vs failure, the need to achieve influences behaviour in a large number of quite diverse situations and because it is a learned motive, there are wide differences among individuals in their past experiences and hence in their motivation with respect of achievement. There is a universal tendency in man to strive, to excel, to succeed and to win and go ahead of others. This is more likely to be learnt by the social customs and education than the inborn. This tendency can be called the 'self assertion' or the 'motive to achieve.' This affects a great many activities of individual and help him in meeting the obstruction which come in the way of achieving of his goal.

Achievement motivation has also been referred to as need for achievement (and abbreviated as N—achievement) is a wish to do well. It refers to an individual who strives to accomplish something, to do his best, to excel others in performance. This involved competition with a standard of excellence. Murray who introduced the concept of need achievement describes personality in terms of psychogenic needs and need achievement is one of them. He argues, psychogenic needs are important in understanding human behaviour.

The tendency which is called need achievement is deep rooted and fixed in human nature. The presence of need achievement can be traced through a great many activities of the individual. Success has become a human goal. It if cannot be attended in one way, it must be attended by another. Supporting this statement. Seidman points out." The feeling of worth each of us has, if we are to become, sure of ourselves, must be proved against and again by achieving. In the most simple and difficult ways we are driven to prove our worth."

It is however, David Mcclelland, who is noted for his work on achievement motivation, says-"If there is anything that all this research has taught me, it is that men can shape their own destiny, that external difficulties and pressures are not merely so important in shaping history as some people have argued. It is how people respond to those challenges that matters and how they respond depends on how strong their concern for achievement is. So the question of what happens to our civilization or to our business community depends quite literally on how much time tens or thousands or even millions of us spend thinking about achievement, about setting moderate achievable goals taking calculated risks, assuming personal responsibility and finding out how well we have loved our job. The answer is up to us."

NOTION OF SELF-CONCEPT

Though several meanings can be assigned to the concept of 'self' but as pointed out by Hall and Lindzey (1957) two of them are important. Firstly, it is used frequently to refer to a person's attitude and feelings about himself and secondly, it is regarded as a group of psychological processes which govern behaviour and adjustment. The first meaning may be called the self as an object, defined since it denotes the persons attitude, feelings, perceptions and evaluation of himself as an object. The second meaning may be called the self as proceess definition. The self is a doer in the sense that it consists of an active group of processes such as thinking remembering and perceiving. Some writers use the term 'ego' for the first, but this distinction has not remained clear and the two terms continue to be used interchangeably in the field of psychology.

Ego is defined, by Symond (1951),' as a group of processes mainly perceiving, thinking and executing a plan of action for attaining satisfaction in response to inner drives', and the self as the ways in which the individual reacts to himself. The self consists of four aspects (a) how a person perceives himself; (b) what he thinks of himself; (c) how he evaluates himself; and (d) how he attempts through various actions to enhance or defend himself.

Mead (1934) setforth a conception of self which has had a strong, impact upon psychological thinking. Mead's self is an object of awareness rather than a system of processes and is a social form of self. It can arise only in a social setting where there is a social communication.

Allport (1961) has defined self-concept as something of which we are immediately aware of. We think of it as the warm, central, private region of our life. As such it plays a crucial part in our consciousness (a concept broader than self), in our personality (a concept broader than consciousness) and in our organism (a concept broader than personality). This it is some kind of core in our being.

This survey of the view of different psychologists regarding the self and ago clearly points out that there is inconsistency in the ways in which self and ego are used by various authors.

Carl Rogers (1951) presented his self theory which is fully developed statement. He refers that self and self concept denotes, "the organised consistent conceptual gestalt composed of perceptions of the characteristics of the 'I' or 'me' and the perceptions of the relationships of the 'I' or 'me' to others and various aspects of life, together with the values attached to these perceptions. It is a gestalt which is available to awareness though not necessarily in awareness. It is fluid and changing gestalt, a process, but any given moment it is a specific entity (Rogrs, 1959)".

The main conceptual ingredient of Rogers, theory according to Hall and Lindzey (1957) are: (a) the organism who is a total individual, (b) the phenomenal field which is totality of experience and (c) the self which is differentiated portion of phenomenal field and consists of a pattern of conscious perceptions and values of 'I' or 'me'. The organism process the following properties such as, (i) it reacts as an organised whole to the phenomenal field in order to satisfy its needs; (ii) it has one basic motive namely to actualize, maintain, and enhance itself; (iii) it may symbolize its experiences so that they become conscious, or it may deny them symbolization so that they remain unconscious, or it may ignore its experiences.

The self which is nuclear concept of Rogers theory, has numerous properties some of which are mentioned here (a) it develops out of organisms interactions with the environment; (b) it may interject the value of other people and receive them in a distorted fashion; (c) the self strives for consistency; (d) the organism behaves in ways that are consistent with the self; (e) experiences that are consistent with the self may change as a result of maturation and learning.

Rogers is credited for his formulation regarding the phenomenal self which have led directly to the making of predictions and to investigate activities in his sense this theory is useful.

After Rogers theory of 'self' many other psychologists also concentrated their attention to phenomena logical view of self and they try to define the concept in terms of capacity to conceptualize himself.

Lolvinger (1970) proposed a personality trait which she defined as the capacity to conceptualize the self, or to 'assume distance' from one self and one's impulses. According to her, it is the manifestation of one's trait in personality inventories that have been described in such terms as facade, test taking defensiveness, response set, social desirability, acquiescence, and personal style.

Recently, Hurlock (1974) spelled out more definite and specific terms what a person "can call his" and what are the structural components which form the self-concept.

According to her, the concept of self has three major components; the perceptual, conceptual and attitudional. The perceptual component is similar to physical self-concept which includes the image of one"s appearance attractiveness and sex appropriateness of body and the importance of different parts of the body. The conceptual component is similar to psychological self concept which relates to the originality of the individual, his abilities and disabilities, his social adjustment and traits of personality. The attitudinal component refers to attitudes of a person about his present status and future prospects, his feelings about his worthiness, his attitude of self esteem, pride and shame. It includes his beliefs, convictions, values, ideals, aspirations, and commitment also.

Lastly, it may be said that the self-concept connotes private experiences and self evaluations which results from an individuals intensely personal private learning. It is essentially private even though it is in part translated into action by most of the things we say and do, by the attitude we express. According to MeCondless (1961) the self-concept maybe thought of as a set of expectancies plus evaluations of area of behaviour with reference to which these expectancies are held. The self has been defined as perceiver and a thing perceived, a knower and a thing that is known.

DEVELOPMENT OF SELF-CONCEPT

An individual is not born with a self-concept but forms one as a result of his experiences and reaction to the environment. As a child grows and develops he learns not only about the world around him but also about himself. He develops capacity to see himself as an object, yet it is not deliberately taught to him by his parents and others concerned about his instruction, from the learning point of view, the self-concept and personal experiences the child has had. It may be observed that the behaviour and the self-concept mutually go on influencing each other.

Lolvinger suggested that ability to form a self concept increases with age, intelligence, education and Socio-economic level. At the lowest point illustrated by the infant, the individual is incapable of self-actualization. As the ability develops, he gradually forms a stereotyped, conventional socially acceptable concept of himself. This stage Lolvinger considers to say typical of adolescence with increasing maturity, the individual progresses beyond such a stereo typed concept to a differentiated and realistic self-concept. At this point he is fully aware of his idiosyncrasies and accepts himself for what he is. According to Lolvinger, many persons fail to reach the final stage i.e. differentiated self concept.

ASPECT OF SELF

Four popular dimensions of self are:

The Perceived Self

This is an individual's concept of the kind of person he is. It is influenced by physical self, physical appearance, dress and grooming by his abilities and dispositions, his values, beliefs and aspirations. By perceptual self is meant the aspect of one's nature, which have been detected and integrated into a pattern, it constitutes the concept or idea of one entertains about one self.

The Real Self

By the real self is meant one's nature with all its potentialities. A person is aware of some aspect but unware of other aspect of his own self. The real self includes what he is aware of and what he is not aware of. It is the perceived self plus unconscious self.

The Social Self

This self as the person thinks others see it. The concept may not correspond with other people's perception of him; nevertheless, it has an important effect on his behaviour.

The Ideal Self

Butler and Haigh (1954) depict the ideal self as the organised conceptual pattern of characteristics and emotional states which an individual consciously holds for himself. The assumption that the individual is able to order his self perception along continuum of values from "what I like to be "to" what I would least like to be".

All aspects of a persons' self-concept may be very similar to each other. Large discrepancies between any two aspects of self spell out a maladjusted personality, showing a little insight into one self and having no self-confidence. The discrepancy between the perceived, sometimes called self-acceptance or self-regard. The discrepancy between perceived and real selves is an index of self-insight. There is a close and linear relationships between discrepancy scores and indices of maladjustment.

The Self System

The self system is composed of formed or forming aspects of an oscillating equilibrium (kelman, 1971) between these aspects of self, there is tensions, friction, and conflict. There are higher order of systems which are either apparently rigid, permanent and formed or dynamic, plastic, impermanent forms.

More generally those different aspects of self are at variance with one another. These variance or discrepancies between the different aspects of self are very important in understanding of an individual. These discrepancies can be between the perceived self and the real self, real self and the ideal self. The difference between the perceived self and ideal self is termed as self acceptance or self-discrepancy. The difference between perceived self and real self is called self insight.

Concept of Intelligence

Human beings have always been intrigued by their own intelligence and the intelligence of mankind. For laymen and teachers alike, intelligence has served as a blanket term to cover all aspects of child's intellectual abilities. Earlier, researchers on such as investiness, imagination and originality, though pointing in the direction of clear difference between intelligence and these other abilities, were of little more theoretical interest.

The extra nature of intelligence had been a disputed topic. People accumulated quite a good number of definitions. But it was unfortunate that no two definitions agreed in themselves. Psychologists, who advance such definitions, were not agreed on a single definition of intelligence, probably because of the differing emphasis which they place on the attributes which can justifiably be regarded as intelligent behaviour. We must look for certain trends behind the various definitions which they advanced. Some psychologists called it as an ability to learn (Buckinghum, Vanwagenen, Calvin), some said it to be an ability of adjustment (Stern, Calvin), others referred it as an ability to abstract thinking (Terman, William Stern, Stoddard, Ravena) sometimes it was defined to be a global capacity measuring several abilities jointly (wechsler, 1958), psychologists like Spearman (1927); Thurstone (1947), Thomson (1948) and Vernon (1951) took recourse to statistical analysis of the results of intelligence testing. They proposed their theories of intelligence on the nature of intelligence. One useful classification of definitions given by Vernon (1960) who decides them into (a) biological, (b) psychological and (c) operational. Briefly the biological definitions stress on adaptation to environment and actions which are of survival values. Psychological definitions are mainly to do with reasoning relational thinking and what terman calls capacity for abstract thinking (Vernon, 1960). Operational definitions are very much the province of the behaviourist school in psychology which makes no assumptions about internal mental processes but only observes the outward manifestation of what is defined as intelligent behaviour. Operational means definable in observable ways.

In spite of these controversies on the nature, intelligence could be measured quite efficiently. Some psychologists compared the nature of intelligence with the nature of electricity. As electricity can be measured accurately without knowing its nature, similarly, it was pleaded that intelligence could be measured precisely.

WHAT RESEARCH SURVEYS CONVEY

In order to have a clear picture of the present state of research which can provide an insight as well as a scope, the researches in the concerned field was reviewed by the investigator. For the sake of clarity and convenience this chapter has been parted into five different headings as given below:

Achievement Motivation as Related to Creativity in Different Groups

It is a general belief that motivation is a vital component of Creativity (Taylor, 1964). In order to explore the relationship between creativity and achievement motivation, McClelland (1956) found that successful scientists like successful salesmen had a higher need for achievement. Eminent Mathematicians in Helson and Crutch field's study (1970) scored more on achievement motivation than average mathematicians. Seventeen ph.D. industrial research chemists were divided by Blast and Stain (1957) into two groups of eight more and nine less creative chemists based on ratings on creativity as obtained from superior colleagues. The more creative were found to be autonomous, striving and devoted than their less creative colleagues. Similar to this finding, Kumar (1978) stated that the creative are more achievement motivated than the non-creative ones.

In a study of personality dynamics of high school seniors, Parloff and Datta (1965) of National Institute of Mental Health found that high creative students as compared to low creative were more ambitious and driving, more independent, autonomous, self-reliant, more efficient and perceptive, more rebellious towards rules and more imaginative.

In India, Raina (1968) compared the high creative and low creative groups of students on certain measures of cognitive abilities, personality, manifest anxiety, academic achievement, socio-economic status by administering MTCT on 500 students of class VIIIth, IXth and Xth of seventeen schools and three educational zones of Rajasthan, high and low creative groups were selected. Analysis of 'F' test and correlational techniques revealed that high creative subject exhibited greater autonomy, achievement, dominance, change and endurance than the low creative subjects.

In a study of female college students aged between 18-21 years, Jawa (1971) obtained significant correlation between creativity and need achievement. High creative girls as compared to low creative were found to have more need for achievement. Similarly, Aaron and Malestha (1972) reported strong relationship between creativity and achievement motivation. Sample of his study consisted of fifty high school boys of two schools of Dharvar. Motivation was assessed in terms of achievement through a standardised TAT, and latest of creativity developed by the investigator was used for necessary fluency and flexibility.

On a sample of 435 B.A. students administering culture fair test of intelligence, scale 3 form A and B, Mandsley personality inventory, incomplete sentence blank Test (by Mukherjee) and Test of creative thinking (by Mehdi), Zargar (1980) found that the high need achievers had a high degree of creativity (verbal) whereas low need achievers had a high degree of non-verbal creativity.

In another study on a sample of 300 male and 300 female students of class IX and X selected from different schools of Agra city from science and arts faculties using achievement motivation test (by Prayag Mehta), verbal test of creative thinking (by Mehdi), level of aspiration test (by Shah and Bhargava) and the Sinha Anxiety scale, Saxena (1981) found that correlation between each and Creativity was significant among the subjects of high and low creative levels. Further, his finding revealed that values, creativity, anxiety and level of aspiration were predictors of achievement for both boys and girls separately.

Conclusion

The survey of researches, in this section, reveals that though achievement motivation of high creative and low creative has been studied but none of the studies reviewed here, intended to assess the achievement motive from different cultural (such as urban, rural and tribal) perspective. Hence, the need of some studies, like the present one, is warranted.

SELF-CONCEPT (PERSONALITY AS RELATED TO CREATIVITY IN DIFFERENT GROUPS

A number of studies have been conducted on creativity on the one hand and different variables of personality on the other hand, such as : Creativity and Extraversion/Introversion (Parmamesh, 1969), Values (Paramesh, 1970 b), Perception (Jawa, 1976) Faminity (Raychandaraa 1970 b) and many other variables of personality including a few studies on self-concept. The researcher has made an attempt to review the available literature on self-concept aspect of personality and creativity.

Studies by Dravdhl and Cattell (1958) on aritiests and writers and Cross *et al* (1967) on creative artists revealed creative persons to be introverted, anxious and having high degree of ego strength. Pogua's (1965) study explored the inter-relationship between creativity and self esteem of 263 students studying in grades four, five, six and revealed a significant relationship between creativity scores and self esteem scores. Welsberg, Springer, Dukes (1965) studying relationship between self concept and creative thinking of two hundred boys and girls selected from a larger group of fifth grade students, found that correlations between creative thinking and self concept were significant in two areas of creative thinking e.g. fluency and elaboration, but no significant relationship was marked between self concept and creativity, flexibility, originality. Sisk (1966) exploring the relationship between self concept and creativity of elementary school children inter-alia observed that high self concept students performed at a significantly higher level on originality and flexibility than low self concept students. The high creative group, as found by Weisberg and Springer (1967), is rated higher than the less creative ones on strength of self image, case of early recall, humour, availability of oedipal anxiety and uneven ego development. The average level of ego strength and emotional stability is distinctly higher for the effective scientific researchers than for general population.

As regard to productive and creative attitude Taft and Gilchrist (1970) in their study reported that students scoring high on both of these aspects see themselves as idealistic —— Gupta (1977) found the following self-concept of high creative pupils in comparison to their low creative pupils as pupils with higher scores on fluency (v) flexibility (v) or originality (v) and creativity (v) were found to have higher scores on perceived real self-concept, ideal self-concept and self acceptance, (b) pupils with higher score on transformation (v) were found to have higher self acceptance : i) a) pupils with higher scores on productive design ability (N.V.) and creative (N.V.) were found to have high ideal self concept and self acceptance, b) pupils with higher scores on complexity (N.V.) Originality were found to have significantly higher self acceptance c) pupils with higher scores on novelty (N.V.) and flexibility (N.V.) were found to have higher ideal self concept, and d) pupils with higher scores on elaboration (N.V.) were found to have lower ideal real self discreancy.

INTELLIGENCE AS RELATED TO CREATIVITY

In recent years many attempts have been made to find out relationship between creativity and many other variables including intelligence. Among the studies on the relationship between creativity and intelligence diversified results have been reported.

STUDIES REFLECTING "POSITIVE RELATIONSHIP

A close relationship between creativity and intelligence was evidenced by Getzels and Jackson (1962). Again a number of studies conducted by Spring belt (1957), Edward *et al* (1965), Hussain and Butcher (1966), Parney and Horrocks (1967), Schlit (1968) senlict *et al* (1965), Parney and Horrocks (1967), Schlit (1968)

Senlict *et al* (1965), Neuringe (1969), Passi (1972), Sharma (1972), and Singh et al (1977) reflected a significantly high correlation between creativity and intelligence. Qureshi (1980) on a sample of 300 girls of high schools and intermediate classes, selected from Firozabad town, administering Mehdi's test of creativity, Group test of Mental Ability (Jalota), STAT (Sharma and Singh, Hindi), Level of Aspiration Inventory (Patel), utilizing analysis of variance od coefficient of correlation, found that intelligence, manifest anxiety and aspiration indicated influence on creativity and its components-fluency, flexibility, originality differently; intelligence appeared to be significantly and positively correlated with creativity. Significant effect of intelligence, avers Jarial (1980), on fluency, originality and total creativity of the students. The high inter correlations among intelligence, academic achievement and creativity, recorded by Yadav (1985), indicated that creativity can be fostered within the individual by providing enriched academic environment. Again Yadav (1987) found significant correlation between I.Q. and creativity.

A positive 'r' ranging from .11 to .73 between intelligence test scores and scores on test of creativity with a mean correlation coefficient of .56 was reported by Ripple and May (1962) . The correlation between creative writing and verbal creativity with all the three scales, Mitchall (1968) found correlation coefficient ranging from .48 to .60 A 'r' of .50 was found by Hattie (1964), Perry (1967), Raina (1968) found the 'r' between TTCT and Mental ability; TTCT and Otis; TTCT and Jalota's test to be .37, .50 and .18 respectively. Ward (1975) on a sample of IV to VI grade students using Wallach-Kogan creativity tests, Mednick's RAT and Lorge Thorndike's I.Q. tests found the 'r' between creativity and intelligence to be .34.

However, Keer and Abraham (1962), Ripple and May (1962). Jackson and Asher (1963), Clark *et al* (1965), Eisenman and Robbinson (1967), Madans (1967), Cropley (1967), Ginsberg and Whittemors (1968), Mehdi (1974,1977), Deshmukh (1979), and Kishore (1981) found significant but low correlation between the two variables among school children.

Interestingly Chadha (1987) found positively significant correlation between creativity and intellectual capacity. Further, his partial correlations between the two variables showed as insignificant 'r' between creativity and intelligence when the effect of school achievement was partialled out.

STUDIES REFLECTING "NO RELATIONSHIP"

Contrary to above findings Anderson (1960) asserted that there is no relationship between I.Q. and divergent production. Wallach and Kogan (1965) may be credited for having demonstrated the distinction between creativity and intelligence. They successfully proved that creativity can be distinguished from intelligence both conceptually and interms of measurement or assessment. Their conclusion have been supported by Fea (1968), Ward (1969) and Child (1970). On a sample of VII and XI grade students using creativity tests patterned after Guilford and Wallach's tests and Ravens progressive matrices, Khire (1971) reported that creativity showed zero correlation with intelligence. High achievers on intelligence reported by Rawat and Agarwal (1977), were not always high achievers on creativity and vice versa. It can be inferred that individuals who are intelligent may not be creative thinkers and highly creative thinkers need not to very intelligent. Raj (1978) on a sample of 610 secondary school pupils in kerala selected by proportionate stratified sampling technique found that all the creativity variables and the cognitive variables discriminated between the students of high intelligences and of low intelligence. The level of creativity did not affect intelligence was evidenced from Bhattacharya's (1978) findings. On the same line Gupta (1980-82) asserted that creativity whether verbal or non-verbal, was independent of intelligence (and socio-economic status). From her factor analysis Glati (1982) affirmed that for creative thinking, creativity and intelligence constituted distinct factors relatively independent of each other. Moran et al (1983) demonstrated that original thinking as measured by Wallach-Kogan tests of creativity was shown to be distinct from intelligence as measured by Wechsler's pre-school and primary scale of intelligence. Hattie and Roggers (1986) proved with certainty that the usual first order factor model that allowed for the estimation of unique covariance between the fluency and originality scores was proposed. Seven data sets were used to compare the fit of this model to the alternative model, whereby the unique covariances were constrained to be zero. The model with unconstrained unique covariences was supported and when this model was used creativity and intelligence were more readily recognised as separate dimensions.

Creative potential, as reported by Persaud and Stimpson (1986), was considered relatively independent of general intelligence, and can be more appropriately measured by divergent production tests. The circle games (C.G.) and Cettell's culture fir intelligence scale-2 (CCFIT) was administered on children in grade 4 (N = 36), 7 (N = 310 and 10 (N=29). Their mean ages wore 10,13 and 16 years respectively. Statistical analysis of data in C.G. was compared between grades 10 and 4 (P< .01) and grades 7 and 4 (P< .05) and in CCFIT pairs of grades (P< .01). Further the results suggested that C.G. and CCFIT were independent measures; Originality contributed most significantly to higher C.G. scores as children grow older. Sansanwal and Jarial (1987) found that there was on significant difference among male students belonging to high and low intelligence groups, with respect to mean fluency, mean flexibility, mean originality and mean total creativity. Examining the original thinking as measured by Wallach-Kogan battery, Milgram at al (1987), on a sample of 41(23 girls and 18 boys) Israeli preschool children found that original thinking was unrelated to Wachsler's preschool intelligence scores.

STUDIES REFLECTING "NEGATIVE RELATIONSHIP"

On a sample of 474 boys drawn from various high schools in two cities of Hyderabad and Secunderabad, using Passi Test of Creativity, Group Test of Mental Ability and High School Personality Questionnaire, interestingly Muddu (1980) recorded that high creative group was found to be negatively correlated (r= -0.096) with intelligence. Relationships between intelligence and fluency (r=0.124), flexibility (r = 0.114), and originality (r = 0.125). Persaud and Stimpson (1986) reported that the correlation between the circle games (C.G.) and Cattell's culture fair intelligence scale - 2 (CCFIT) ranged from low negative to low positive.

ASSUMED FACTORS AFFECTING RELATIONSHIP

Jarial (1982) after reviewing half-a-century (1930-1982) of empirical researches on the relationship between creativity and intelligence concluded that, creativity and intelligence are two distinctive mental abilities. They are related to certain extent, but the nature and extent of their relationship depends upon different factors, such as, the definition of creativity, sample studied, instrument used, and the I.Q. range of the subjects. Though intelligence is an essentiality to creativity, but it is not the only requirement. As such, highly intelligent persons need not always be highly creative. At certain I.Q. level creativity shows zero correlation with intelligence.

Conclusions

However, from his survey of related literature the investigator concluded that the relationship between creativity and intelligence is controversial, uncertain, speculative and of varying degree.

DESCRIPTION OF THE MEASURES USED: ACHIEVEMENT MOTIVATION TEST BY MOHAN (1971)

The Achievement Motivation test (1971) constructed by Mohan was used for collection of data on achievement motivation (n-ach) of the subjects.

Test Content

It is a TAT type projective test containing five pictures of different situations prepared on the lines of McClelland and Atkison (1958). The pictures are drawn and sketched in back and white on a thick poster size drawing sheet 20" to 15" size which could be displayed like a poster to a group of normal size class in Indian setting. Picture No. 1 was common for both boys and girls depicting to the class-room situation. Picture numbers 2,3,4 and 5 are separate for boys and girls describing library, technical or laboratory, sports and music situation respectively. In all, there are five pictures prepared on the pattern of McClelland et al (1958). According to the test instruction the subjects were asked to write a story after properly seeing the picture within a stipulated time.

Reliability

The reliability coefficients were obtained by Mohan (1971) different methods as indicated below:

Sl. No.	*Method of Reliability*	*N*	*Reliability Coefficient*
1.	Test- retest	66	.41
2.	Inter scorer	50	.84 to .91
3.	Score-rescore	50	.82

Validity

Regarding validity McClelland (1955), Morgan (1953), Murray (1933), etc. have found this test highly correlated with such relevant tests.

Applicability

A wealth of research data on achievement motivation have been produced by David McClelland and his co-workers. From their extensive research they asserted that like other forms of human motivation, achievement motivation can best be studied in the realm of fantasy. As the achievement motivation test constructed by Mohan (1971) is highly valid, reliable and projective measure of achievement motivation, it was preferred to any verbal scale of measuring n-Ach, because it is prepared in Indian setting.

PERSONALITY WORDLIST (PWL) BY DBO (1971)

The personality Word List (PWL) was constructed by Deo 1971). It was used in the present study as a measure of self-concept of the subjects.

Test Content

Personality word list contains 90 adjectives of everyday use, out of which 56 are positive and 34 are negative adjectives. It is a self rating scale than a check list to be rated by the subjects on a five point scale; the five points being "very much like this" "Much like this", uncertain," "not much like this", and "not at all like this".

Reliability

The reliability was estimated by test-retest method. For the 15 days interval, the reliability coefficient came out to be .89 (N = 595). Taking different time interval from 15 days to 3 $^1/_2$ months, the reliability coefficient ranged from .62 to .86 (Singh, 1996-67). The correlations between consistency scores ranged from .84 to .98. These values indicate a high degree of consistency. It also did not mark any pronounced difference in the self-concepts of individual over these periods. This proves that the Personality World List (PWL) gives a stable and reliable measure of self-concept.

Validity

For obtaining the convergent validity, another tool namely self concept list which had also been standardised was utilized by the author of the test. The table showing convergent and discriminant validities for perceived self (manual p-10) revealed the convergent correlations between the same dimensions in all cases are higher than the discriminant correlations, thus providing the validity of the instrument. The convergent validity was determined by Singh (1965) which ranged from .40 to .65.

Applicability

Out of various self-concept tests PWL was selected by the investigator for the present problem because (i) it has high reliability and validity (ii) it is easy for quick measuring and scoring, (iii) the same test can be used to measures other dimensions of self - concept with the same tool to be administered on different occasions.

MEASURE OF INTELLIGENCE: CATTELL'S CULTURE FAIR TEST OF INTELLIGENCE

Form A, Factor 'G' (1965)

Nature of the Scale : Cattele's Culture Fair Intelligence Test, as the title suggests, is a culture fair tests measure individual difference in intelligence in a manner designed to reduce, as much as possible, the influenced of verbal fluency, cultural climate, and educational level. The tests can be administered individually or in a group. Cattell's tests of intelligence are non-verbal in nature and require only the examinees to perceive relationships in shares and figures.

Content of the Scale: It consists three scales for three different age groups. For the present study scale II was used, because this scale suits best to the age group 14 + taken for the investigation. This scale contains four subtests involving different perceptual tasks, so that the composite intelligence measure avoids spurious reliance on a single skill. Those four subtests are : Series, Classification, Matrices and conditions, having 46 items in total. A sample of each subtest is briefly described as below.

Series

It is the first of four subtests. In this, the subject is presented with an incomplete, progressive series. His task is to select, from among the choices provided, the answer which best continues the series.

Classification

This is the second of the four subtests containing the scale. Here in this subtest i.e. classification, the subject is presented with five figures. The subject must select one which is different from the other four.

Matrices

This is the third subtest of the total scale. In this subtest the task of the subject is to correctly complete the design or the matrix presented at the left of each row.

Conditions

This is the final subtest of the total scale. Conditions (Topology) requires the individual to select, from the five choices provided, the one which duplicates the conditions given in the far left box.

Reliability and Validity

The test-retest reliability coefficients ranged from .67 to .76 and the concept validity and concrete alidity were .81 and .70 respectively.

Appicability

The selection and use of a psychometric measure, for research point of view, based not only on its reliability and validity but should also based on the understanding of nature of the sample, besides the purpose of the study. The sample of the present study consists of adolescents of Western Orissa, whose mother tongue is Oriya. As the test is a non-verbal one, the possibility of the effect of language is not there in the test performance. Secondly, as the test itself is a culture fair measure, the effect of culture is also minimised in test performance. Hence the selection and utilization of Culture fair test of intelligence of Cattell is justified.

PRESENT STUDY CREATIVITY AND ACHIEVEMENT MOTIVATION

While identifying creative talent psychologists do stress on personality characteristics and motivtional aspect. Achievement motive or motive to achieve is one of the important personality variables responsible in life's success to a great extent. Hence, its significance in creative performance can not be ignored or under estimated. Creativity research in relation to achievement motivation will prove it self quite stimulating and promising.

"A STUDY OF THE DIFFERENCES IN ACHIEVEMENT MOTIVATION OF HIGH AND LOW CREATIVE ADOLESCENTS"

Definition of the term used:
Achievement Motivation

The achievement motivation or need to achieve is an index of subjects striving to success, compete with others with a standard of excellence. Achievement motivation is estimated from subjects' expression to Mohan's Tat type achievement motivation test (1971). Mohan's Tat pictures served as timuli for the subjects to write a story which would reflect their concern for competition, standard of excellence and long term involvement. Several indices are there to estimate subjects scores on achievement motivation.

High Creative

This indicates the status of the subjects in relation to the group on the variable creativity. Subjects who scored above Q3 (third qauartile) or 75 percent of the cases on total creativity scores were termed as high creative.

In others words, the subjects belonging to the highest 25 per cent of the cases on total creativity scores were termed as high creative (H.C.).

Low Creative

Subjects who scored below the Q1 (first quartile) or 25th percentile of the total scores were reported to as low creative. In other words, the subjects belonging to the lowest 25 per cent cases on total creativity scores were termed as low creative (L.C.).

Urban Group

In the present study urban adolescents referred to those secondary school students (Class IX) belonging to town area of four districts namely—Sambalpur, Sundargarh, Bolangir and Kalahandi of Western Orissa. Subjects were drawn mainly from Govt. Boys and Girls Secondary Schools of the above mentioned districts.

Rural Group

Rural adolescents, in the present study referred to those subjects belonging to the village area living away from the town culture and atmosphere of Sambalpur, Sundargarh, Bolangir and Kalahandi districts. Most of the rural schools were private ones, a few were govt. aided. Almost all the rural schools were co-educational with only one exception which was a girls school.

Tribal Group

The tribal adolescents in the present study referred to those randomly selected subjects who were admitted to secondary schools run by Tribal Rural Welfare Deptt. (T.R.W.) Govt. of Orissa. Out of the total TRW schools majority were located in village area one school located in jungle area and a few in town area and town culture.

Objective

4. To study the differences in achievement motivation of high and low creative adolescents.

Hypothesis

H_4: Theere is no significant difference between high and low creative adolescents so far as achievement motivation is concerned.

Methodology and Procedure

Sample

In total 580 randomly drawn subjects of class IX from urban, rural and tribal (204 Ss urban, 213 Ss rural, 163 Ss tribal) constituted the sample of the present study. A detailed picture of the selection of the small is presented earlier in third chapter in Label No. 3.1 and area of sample is located in Figure No. 3.1

Instruments Used

i) To assess the creative potential of the subjects the Wallach-Kogan Tests of Creativity adopted in Oriya by Tripathy (1979) was issued.

ii) To assess the achievement motivation of the subjects Achievement Motivation test by Mohan (1971) was used. The justification of using this test and description of the test is presented in this chapter earlier.

Data Collection

The data for the present study were collected by the researcher personally from schools of all the four selected districts of Western Orissa. Tests of Creativity and achievement motivation were administered by the investigator as per the procedure laid down in test manual.

Statistical Technique Employed

In the present study several statistical techniques employed to analyse the collected data. To test the hypothesis based on objective of the study different statistical treatment was needed.

Percentile particularly 75th and 25th percentile were calculated on subjects scores on creativity to categorise high creative and low creative.

Again, descriptive analysis such as Means, SD's and 't' ratios and testing the significant difference between means were workout to compare the groups-urban, rural and tribal on achievement motivation.

RESULTS AND DISCUSSION

Creativity and Achievement Motivation

In order to examine whether high creative and low creative groups differ significantly in terms of achievement motivation. The high creative and low creative students were identified on the basis of their performance in creativity measures. Adolescents whose creativity scores were above (third quartile) were categorised as high creative group (H.C.) and adolescents whose creativity scores were below (first quartile) were termed as low creative group (L.C.). Again, means and standard deviations of high and low creative groups on achievement-motivation measure (achievement-motivation scores) was computed and compared, the result of which is given in Table 4.2.1.

It is observed from the table 4.2.1. that the mean achievement-motivation scores of high creative (H.C.) and low creative (L.C.) adolescents differ significantly in all the cases of urban, rural and tribal sub-cultures. The obtained 't' ratios 8.48, 4.26 and 2.38 (between urban high and low creative, rural high and low creative, tribal high and low creative respectively) are significant P< .01 for first two cases and P< . 05 for tribal high and low creative cases. It means that high creative adolescents differ significantly from low creative ones in terms of achievement-motivation and in all the sub-cultures high creative adolescents possess greater achievement motivation than the low creative ones.

It may be interpreted that it is the higher achievement motive or need achievement which promotes them to show their creative performance. Earlier, several studies, Jawa (1971), Malestha (1972) and Sexena (1981), reported similar findings which provide much useful data about the strength of relationship between creativity and achievement motivation (need to achieve).

Creativity and Self-Concept

As mentioned earlier Psychologists, while identifying creative talent, do stress on personality characteristics among other things. Self-concept, being one of the important aspects of personality, is vital for life's success and human behaviour including creativity. Hence, its significance in creative performance can not be ignored or underestimated. Creativity research in relation to self-concept (perceived) will prove itself quite stimulating and promising.

"A STUDY OF THE DIFFERENCES IN SELF-CONCEPT OF HIGH AND LOW CREATIVE ADOLESCENTS"

TABLE 4.2.1

Mean, Standard Deviating and 't' Values For Urban, Rural and Tribal Adolescents of High and Low Creative Groups on Achievement Motivation

Groups		*N*	*Mean*	*SD*	*'t'*
Urban	H.C.	50	1.82	1.57	8.48 **
	L.C.	46	1.15	1.18	
Rural	H.C.	53	2.42	1.85	4.26 **
	L.C.	53	1.10	1.32	
Tribal	H.C.	42	1.26	1.23	2.38 *
	L.C.	42	.74	.69	

H.C. = High Creative * Significant at .05 level

L.C. = Low Creative ** Significant at .01 level

Definition of the Terms Used:

Self-concept

Self-concept (perceived) reflects how the subjects perceive themselves. It was estimated by subjects obtained scores on Personality Word List of P.Deo (1971).

High Creative

This indicates the status of the subjects in relation to the group on variable creativity. Subjects who scored above Q3 (third quartile) or 75th percentile of the total scores were identified as high creative. In other words, the subjects belonging to the highest 25 per cent of the cases on total creativity scores were termed as high creative (H.C.).

Low Creative

Subjects who scored below the Q1 (first quartile) or 25th percentile of the total scores were reported to as law creative. In other words, the subjects belonging to the lowest 25 per cent cases on total creativity scores were termed as law creative.

Urban Group

In the present study urban adolescents referred to those secondary school students (class IX) belonging to town area of four districts namely—Sambalpur, Sundargarh, Bolangir, Kalahdndi of Western Orissa. Subjects were drawn mainly from Govt. Boys and Girls Secondary Schools of the above mentioned districts.

Rural Group

Rural adolescents, in the present study, referred to those subjects belonging to the village area living away from town culture and atmosphere of Sambalpur, Sundargarh, Bolangir and Kalahandi districts. Most of the rural schools were co-educationer with one exception which was a girls school.

Tribal Group

The Tribal adolescents in the present study referred to those randomly selected subjects who were admitted to secondary schools run by Tribal Rural Welfare Deptt. (TRW), Govt of Orissa. Out of the total TRW schools majority were located in village area. One school located in jungle and a few in town area and town culture.

Objective

5. To study the self-concept of high and low creative adolescents.

Hypothesis

H_5: There is no significant difference between high and low creative adolescents so far as the self-concept is concerned.

Methodology and Procedure

Sample

On the whole 580 randomly drawn subjects of class IX from urban, rural and tribal area (204 Ss urban, 213 Ss rural and 163 Ss tribal) constituted the sample of the present study.

Instruments Used

i) To assess the creative potential of the subjects the Wallach-Kogon test of creativity adopted in Oriya by Tripathy (1979) was used.
ii) To assess the self-concept of the subject Personality Word List by P.Deo (1971) was used.

Data Collection

The data for the present investigation were collected by the investigator personally from schools of all the four selected districts of Western Orissa. Test of creativity and personality word list were administered by the investigator as per procedure laid down in the tests manual.

Statistical Technique Applied

Percentile particularly 75th and 25th percentile were calculated on subjects scores on creativity to categorise high creative and low creative.

Again, descriptive analysis such as means, SD's, and 't' ratios and testing the significant difference between means were workout to compare the groups-urban, rural and tribal on self-concept.

RESULTS AND DISCUSSIONS

Creativity and self-concept

In order to examine whether high creative and low creative groups differ significantly in terms of self-concept. The high creative and low creative subjects were selected on the basis of their performance on creativity measures. The procedure of selection of high creative and low creative has already been explained earlier in this chapter (page 37). Again means and standard deviations of high and low creative groups on self-concept measure was computed, compared, the results of which are given in Table 4.2.2.

It is observed from the Table 4.2.2. that mean perceived self concept scores of high creative (H.C.) and low creative (L.C.) adolescents differ significantly in the cases of urban and rural sub-cultures. The obtained 't' ratios 3.39 and 3.21 (between urban high and low creative and rural high and low creative respectively) are significant P. 01 for the above two cases.

It means that high creative adolescents differ significantly from low creative ones in terms of self concept. In other words in urban and rural sub-culture high creative adolescents possess higher self concept than the low creative ones. This indicates the fact that higher/greater perceived self concept contributes significantly to creative performance. Earlier researcher like Gupta (1977) supported this finding.

However, so far as the mean perceived self concepty scores of tribal high and low creative adolescents are concerned surprisingly tribal low creative adolescents scored higher than tribal high creative though the differences are not significant. However, many more studies are required to conclude finally the nonsignificant differences between tribal high and low creative adolescents. But for the present study various statistical and other inherent factors and reasons including self perception might be responsible for gaining non-significant differences.

Thus, the fifth hypothesis of no difference is partially accepted. Urban high creative and low creative and rural high creative and low creative g groups differ significantly from one another on perceived self concept. Only tribal high and low creative groups do not differ significantly which proves that the tribal low creative are as higher as their high creative counterparts on perceived self concept.

Creativity as Related to Intelligence

A natural question arising out of special efforts to assess creativity as an independent dimension in the intellectied domain is with regard to its relationship with intelligence which is supposed to underline mental activities. Surveys of available related literature reveals that the nature and the extent relationship between creativity and intelligence is speculative, uncertain and of varying degree. Hence, its proper study is needed to arrive at certain conclusion.

"A STUDY OF THE RELATIONSHIP BETWEEN CREATIVITY AND INTELLIGENCE"

Definition of the terms used:

High Creative

It indicates the standing of the subjects in relation to group on the variable creativity. Subjects who scored above Q3 (third quartile) or 25th percentile of the total scores were identified as high creative. In other words, the subjects belonging to the highest 25 per cent of the cases on the total creativity scores were termed as high creative (H.C.).

Low Creative

Subjects who scored below the Q1 (first quartile) or 25th percentile of the total scores were reported to as low creative (L.C.).

Intelligence

Intelligence of the subjects was measured by Cattell's Culture Fair

Table 4.2.2
Mean, Standard Deviating and 't' Values For Urban, Rural and Tribal Adolescents of High and Low Creative Groups on Self concept

Groups		*N*	*Mean*	*SD*	*'t'*
	H.C.	52	131.20	26.96	
Urban					3.39 **
	L.C.	39	107.06	37.83	
	H.C.	49	134.09	28.98	
Rural					4.26**
	L.C.	46	114.48	30.43	
	H.C.	41	116.29	18.50	
Tribal					.98 N.S.
	H.C.	39	121.55	28.20	

H.C. = High Creative ** Significant at .01 level

L.C. = Low Creative

Test of Intelligence ('g') scale - II. It is a non-verbal culture - free measure of intelligence. Subjects were supposed to select the most accurate right response out of the choices given against each test item.

Urban Group

In the present study urban adolescents referred to those secondary school students (class IX) belonging to town area of four selected districts namely—Sambalpur, Sundargarh, Balangir and Kalahandi of Western Orissa. Subjects were drawn mainly from Govt. Boys and Girls schools of above mentioned districts.

Objective

6. To study the relationship between creativity and intelligence.

Hypothesis

H_6: There is no significant relationship between creativity and intelligence.

METHODOLOGY

Sample

200 urban subjects constituted he sample of the present study. The subjects belong to the town areas of four districts namely Sambalpur, Sundargarh, Bolangir and Kalahand of Western Orissa. Subjects were drawn mainly from Govt. Boys and Girls High schools of above mentioned districts.

Instruments Used:

i) Wallach-Kogan Test of creativity adopted in Oriya by Tripathy (1979).
ii) Cattell's Culture Fair Test of Intelligence Scale-II.

Data Collection

The data for the present study were collected by the researcher personally from the urban area of all the four selected districts of Western Orissa. Test of creativity and Caitell's Culture Fair test of intelligent scale were administered by the investigator as per procedure laid down in the tests manual.

Statistical Technique Employed

Coefficient of correlation (r) was calculated with the help of Pearson's Product Moment method.

Results and Interpretation

Creativity and Intelligence

For this purpose finally scores on different components of creativity (viz. verbal, figural and composite) and intelligence (Non-verbal) of 200 urban subjects were taken into consideration to arrive at the conclusion regarding the nature and extent of relationship between creativity and intelligence. The coefficient of correlation (r) was calculated with the help of Pearson's Product Moment method. The coefficient of correlation between different components of creativity and intelligence are given in Table 4.2.3

Table 4.2.3
Correlation (r) Between components of Creativity (verbal, figural and composite) and intelligence for Total Urban Simple (n=200)

Variables	*Coefficient of Correlation 'r'*
Verbal Creativity and Intelligence	.152 *
Figural Creativity and Intelligence	.140 *
Composite Creativity and Intelligence	.162 *

* Significant at .05 level

It is observed from the Table 4.2.3 that the correlation 'r' between components of creativity (verbal, figural and composite) and non-verbal intelligence is significant but low. The obtained 'r' is .152, .140 and .162 (between verbal creativity and intelligences, figural creativity and intelligence; compositve creativity and intelligence respectively) are significant P< .05 for all the cases. Again the table reveals that the coefficients of correlation (r) between verbal creativity and intelligence is higher than that of figural creativity and intelligence.

It means this is indicative of the fact that creativity and intelligence are correlated but the relation is not so high. This indicates that though intelligence is an essentially to creativity but is not the only requirement as such highly intelligent need not be highly creative. Earlier several studies Jackson and Asher (1963), Cropley (1967). Mehdi (1974) and (1977), Deshmukh (1979) Kishore (1981) reported similar findings.

Thus, the 6th hypothesis of 'no relationship' between creativity and intelligence is rejected. Hence, creativity and intelligence are correlated to each other.

5

Development of Creativity

INTRODUCTION

This chapter is devoted to implications of the study more specially from — i) Socio-cultural, ii) Guidance, iii) Parental and iv) educational point of view. The findings of the study have a message for every person ; community workers, guidance workers, parents, social workers and teachers who have the hope in these growing children who are the future nation builders. The findings of the study which have appertain implications are discussed below;

Socio-cultural Implications :

It is found from the present study that among the urban adolescents, girls are found to be more creative than the boys whereas the same trend is missing in case of rural adolescents. Among the rural adolescents rural boys are found to be remarkably high creative that the rural girls (particularly on verbal 1 and composite creativity.) Girls in rural cultural background fail to show their creative potential as their male counterparts, though the superiority of girls over the boys in creative potential is evident in urban culture. Socio-psychological and cultural variables play a predominant role in most of the human behaviour including creativity. The psychological safety and freedom social reinforcement and status that females of urban society enjoy is different from females of rural and tribal culture. Role playing is another such socialization process. It is observed that in rural society people attach negative values for ladies to be independent, bold, unconventional free whereas the same traits in girls are accepted even valued in urban culture. On the other hand rural society expects the female to be submissive, dependent, conventional rule found as these are feminine virtues. The traits (characteristics) considered as negative for rural females are being found in urban females which are conducive for creative growth and expression. Our common observation reveals that society of Western Orissa impose certain conventional restriction and disciplinary control which hamper their verbal expression. The more the Oriya rural society encourage the girls to be free, sportive, natural, to remain away from traditional rules, restriction and values the more there are chances for girls to be constructive and creative. Hence, the society of western Orissa needs to be more opened, free, democratic and Unconventional in order to foster creativity in rural girls. It also demands a change in the social expectation of girls from parents, elderly members of the society and teachers as well.

It is also found that in all the urban, rural and tribal samples high creatives, in general, possess higher achievement motivation as compared to their low creative ones. It can be said that the high creative adolescents are distinguished by their higher achievement need motivation. Psychological and sociological analysis of achievement motivation (need) reveals that achievement motivation, as a learned motive, is fostered by socio-cultural values, attitudes, habits from the vary childhood. Hence, the responsible members of the society should recognise the socially valued need i.e. achievement motivation and foster the same among the aspiring children. So that in the long run the children will be in a position to how their creative spark in their chosen field of endeavour.

The study also revealed that high creative adolescents in urban and rural societies possess higher perceived self concept than their low creative counterparts. As self-concept is being shaped by past experiences, present status and future expectation. The members of the society can do a lot in fostering the positive and higher self-concept in the growing children.

GUIDANCE IMPLICATION

It is indicated through the results of the present research that urban adolescents, in general, are more creative than their rural counterparts. Again, it is found that sex difference in creativity favouring girls among the urban adolescents is a significant factor. The superiority of urban over the rural and rural boys over the rural girls in creative potential can be eliminated through the efforts made by guidance workers or school counsellors as social workers with the cooperation of teachers in the school. School guidance workers or counsellors through parent teacher association (PTA) in the school can focus light on the parent/teacher's role their treatment, provision or opportunity made available in home and school can make or mar the pupil's creative potential. Hence, it has the guidance implication.

Again, as evident from the study high creative subjects are adolescents having higher achievement motivation. Thus, achievement motive is an indication creativeness. Guidance workers or school counsellors, through P.T.A. can focus light on the socially valued and prized human need i.e. achievement motive and thus help parents as well as teachers to remote the achievement need in the aspiring children.

Likewise self-concept of the students can be enhanced by the parents and teachers with the cooperation of guidance workers in providing realistic goals.

Implications for Parents

As mentioned earlier the superiority of urban girls over the urban boys is evident from the findings of the study. Further it reveals that in rural sample it is found that girls are inferior to boys in creative potential.

This may be due to socio-cultural factors of Western Orissa. Here in this case rural parents have to take a responsible role in promoting verbal freedom of expression and action especially for girls. For stimulating and nurturing creativity of rural girls, they should get psychological safety and psychological freedom which are basic to creative expression. Child rearing practices; parent-child relationship free, democratic and non-evaluative child care are some of the crucial factors that parents should keep in mind for developing the creativity in their growing children. Again, parents have to bring a change in the promotion of sex role expectancy.

In figural and composite creativity also tribal girls are not so creative as their tribal boys. Thus, sex difference in creativity is prominent among tribal adolescents. For this parents have to take an important role in promoting creativity among the girls.

As pointed out earlier, it is evident from the study that high creative adolescents age adolescents having high achievement motivation. Achievement motivation being socio-cultural based needs is resulted from rewards and punishment of specific behaviour hence, there is possibility of raising it. Parents in the family can create atmosphere in which the child feels it is rewarding to achieve the excellence in the field is rally worthy. Thus parents can foster achievement need/motivation in the developing children through approving, valuing and rewarding achievement oriented behaviour in their children which further provide chances, for them, to be more creative.

It is clear from the results of the study that high creative adolescents, in general, possess higher self-concept. Parents can foster higher and positive self concept in their developing children though their encouraging behaviour represented by child-rearing practice, parent-child interaction and understanding the child sympathetically. The more the parents will be able to enhance positive and higher self concept in children the more they have chances of being creative.

EDUCATION IMPLICATION

The last but not the least implication of the study is educational in nature. As stated earlier the study reveals that urban adolescents are more creative than the rural ones and among the rural adolescents, boys are more creative than the girls. This disadvantage position of rural adolescents in general and among the rural adolescents, girls in particular can be compensated through a quality of education. The school climate, teachers interests, inclination and role non-evaluative stress free atmosphere, democratic and optimistic attitude of the teacher, teaching methodology, techniques of asking questions provide the students psychological safety and freedom which will go a long way promoting the creativity in children. Hence, its implication in the field of education in general and rural and tribal education in particular can not be underestimated.

The study also reveals that creative adolescents are those who posses high-level achievement motivation. Thus one can say, it is the higher achievement motivation which is one of the significant conditions of highly creative individuals. Since achievement motivation is a learned notice, the achievement motivation of the students can be raised through education and required training. In teaching learning situation, teachers, administrators can facilitates achievement motive through understanding, appreciating, rewarding achievement oriented behaviour in the students.

It is also evident that high creative adolescents, in general, possess higher self-concept. As self-concept is formed by past experience, present status and future aspiration. The school can improve the self-concept of the students by providing positive experience in and realistic expectation for the growing children.

Research Needs

INTRODUCTION

This chapter purports to focus on research perspective and its implications for action. This chapter also includes guidelines for perspective creativity researchers.

Delimitations of the Study

The present study was confirmed to :

i) The subjects of class IX of urban, rural and tribal areas of Western Orissa. It included four districts namely Sambalpur, Sundargarh, Bolangir and Kalahandi.
ii) Those tribal students who have been admitted to schools run by Tribal-Rural Welfare Deptt. of Govt. of Orissa.
iii) The relationship between intelligence and creativity on urban subjects, and
iv) Administration of various tests on tribal subjects in non-tribal (Oriya) language.

RECOMMENDATION FOR FURTHER RESEARCH

On the basis of thought over the findings of the present study and the gaps found during the process of research, reported in this study, the following are some of the potential areas which need attention for further study :

i) The present investigation was confined to secondary school children only, whereas earlier and later phase of school children could not be possibly studied, which can be considered as important areas of investigation. Moreover secondary school children of Orissa can be compared with neighbouring states or elsewhere to observe whether similar trends of results could be obtained.

ii) Further, in the present study the trial sample consists of secondary school students under the Tribal Rural welfare (TRW) scheme ,Govt. of orissa, where students are living in an impair environment (than the real tribal home background) of residential schools. So studies of this sort may be conducted on their actual tribal back-ground which may adequately reveal the effect of socio-cultural factors.

ii) From the present study it is evident that in urban culture sex difference in creativity was found favouring girls. Whereas in rural and tribal culture the reverse was found. So further study is needed to identify the factors socio-cultural, anthropological, and psychological that are responsible in case of urban girls in stifling creativity. So that it will be a great boon to the society.

iii) Further researches can also be taken in spotting psycho-socio-cultural factors responsible for verbal creativity and the same in case of figural creativity in urban, rural, and tribal culture.

iv) It was also found that high achievement is a prerequisite for creative performance. So studies intending to develop achievement need in students are of great value which can guide the parents in the family, teachers in the schools and adults in the society in promoting achievement need in their pupils through media like socialization, acculturation, education and training.

v) Last but not the least recommendation is that besides the selected instruments (tools) used in the present study one can select other suitable valid and reliable measures for further researches. It is always ideal to employ instruments developed in local language.

With reference to measures of creativity, creativity research can be taken by using different and varied measures of creativity including non-testing techniques like bio-graphical measures to have the convincing data from the subjects about different components of creativity.

These are simply suggestions for further exploration and certainly not the final project, because these can be outcomes of the investigations like the present one. Although there are immense possible ways to carry out research with theoretical and practical implications, it is beyond the scope of this work to suggest designs of such studies. But the investigator, wishes to state the importance of this area which will contribute towards the field of education and psychological research.

ANNEXURE

A Sample Study

A Study of the Creative Potential Achievement Motivation and Self-concept of Urban Rural and Tribal Adolescents

The Context

It is essential that every nation should feel concerned about its potential human resources. It has been observed by specialists that a country shall not be able to sustain economic growth unless all the reserves of creative potential in population are actually sought out and attracted into the needed educational channels. Further, if education to-day is to give something to our future citizen; it is not knowledge or information alone, nor the certificate nor even some of the practical skills which they develop and use in day-to day problems of life; but a trained intellect which would enable them to adjust and readjust themselves in the fast changing world in which they live to-day. Creative thinking too, as has been shown, gets stultified when not properly cared for and stimulated (Mehdi, 1977). If deplorable waste of creative potential is to be prevented and if the creative and talented are not to chose the path of delinquency, mental illness or at best a life of majority and moralised potentialities, then it becomes essential that creative potential be identified and cultivated. Hence, the imperativeness of research work in the field of creativity so as to provide humanity with productive ideas to stimulate creativity (Kothari Commission, 1966).

The importance of the study can be recognised by focusing light on different significant values.

India, one of the largest countries of the world, contains about 98 crores of people speaking more than a dozen languages, following several religions, living in divers geographical climates and terrains. A majority of these people live in rural areas, some live in tribal areas and comparatively a very small section lives in Urban area. Marked differences are obtained among these urban, rural and tribal people on socio-economic standing possibilities and incentives opened for them, social instruction, child rearing practices, social values and the senses of appreciation which finally determine the socio-cultural group enjoys, may prove a limitation for another group or vice-versa. The development of human abilities is the function of the constituent of the body or brain on the one hand and experiences and perceptions obtained from socio-cultural conditions on the other. Thus, creativity, as one of the abilities, is culture-bound. A creative act in a culture, might well be non-creative in another.

Anderson and Anderson (1969) who gathered data from a large number of children of eight countries found that there exists large and significant differences consistent with their hypotheses about the impact of culture on creativity. Emphasizing the prominence of culture from behaviourable stand point Sapir (1934) writes, human behaviour may be studied in terms of culture of the group as a whole and psychic organization of the individual himself, and employment of culture and individual perspectives upon the same collected data. Creative potential, avers Gordan (1961), seeks its maximal actualization within the environmental condition characterised by psychological safety and psychological freedom, socio-cultural influence. Discussing the importance of culture in nuturance and development of creative potential, Rollomay (1969) very succinctly observed that you can never localize creativity as a subjective phenomenon, you can never study it in terms of what goes in a person..... For what is occurring is always a process, a doing, specially a process interrelating a person and his world. Such are the powerful influences of culture in the promotion of creative development and functioning. It is because of these influences that the nature and number of creative production showed great variations among the cultures (kroaber, 1944). Since culture has such a pronounced role in the development of creativity, the understanding and study of culture in relation to this important functioning has its own right for research.

Guidance worker or school counsellors helping students in educational problems generally use intelligence measure but their growing awareness in the area of creativity suggests them to employ creativity measures also in solving academic problems. It is perhaps because this creativity measures (TTCT), asserted Swass (1981), should be used in students for educational guidance. Understanding and helping the students in relation to any behaviour comprising creativity and intelligence, requires the study of their socio-cultural background because abilities develop in relation to physical constituent of the individual and practices and experiences acquired from socio-cultural environment to which the individual is exposed.

Parents should realise the fact that poor quality of schooling coupled with disadvantageous home background accentuates the effect of socio-cultural and academic deprivation that has a detrimental effect on verbal and non-verbal creative thinking abilities (Ahmad and Joshi, 1978). The wide cultural differences in the form of urban, rural and tribal regions and sex role promotion in the form of male or female or son or daughter represented in creative potential, achievement motivation and self-concept of the children is evident from several studies. Hence, the significance of the present study is equally recognised for parental value.

Environment exerts, as has been mentioned earlier, a great influence upon the child. The school where he spends a considerable time and gets formal education assumes importance in shaping his abilities (Sharmas, 1979). Creativity can be fostered within the individuals by providing enriched academic environment. Education can do a great deal in promoting creative performance, if perhaps not in producing the abilities themselves. But the education is too bookish and mechanical, stereotyped and rapidly uniformed that it does not cater to the different aptitudes of pupils. The stress on examination the over crowded syllabus, the method of teaching lack of proper material amenities tend to make education a burden rather than a joyous experience to the bound mind (Secondary Education Commission, 1952-53) and naturally does very little to exploit the value potential of individuals. Already faced with alarming rate of wastage and stagnation and problems like 'massilliteracy', 'brain-drain' and 'malnutrition' no one can simply close his eyes to the tremendous lapse that results in our failure to identify and develop, in our youth, the limit of their creative potential. This point has also been emphasized in the report of Education Commission (1966) which says, 'Even the talent that enters schools and succeeded in climbing the educational ladder does not flourish fully because it has not discovered sufficiently early, and is often studying in poor school.

It is a fact that creativity, like other personality traits, is distributed normally in the population and there is every possibility to be creative in one's own fields. But it would be apt to quote Stoddard (1959) in this connection that the urge to inquire to invent, to perform is stifled in millions of school children, now growing up, who do not get above rate learning or at least do not stay above it.

Recognising, understanding and valuing creativity from socio-cultural context is much more important as socio-cultural conditions favour or hamper creativity in the young children. The disadvantaged children have a significantly low creativity score in comparison to their advantaged counterparts (Singh, 1980). However, optimistically Sultana (1980) viewed that socio-cultural disadvantage retards the development of both verbal non-verbal creativity but the deficiency can be overcome by a quality education. From educational stand point, it is a matter of vital importance that better environment be provided to students to blossom and it is here that the role of the teachers in helping to foster creativity among school going children needs to be emphasized most (Bardrinath and Satyanarayan, 1978-79). Hence, research work in this area will be quite informative, stimulating and promising. This theoretical background provided as insight to the investigator to study the problem which is stated below:

STATEMENT OF THE PROBLEM

"A STUDY OF THE CREATIVE POTENTIAL ACHIEVEMENT MOTIVATION AND SELF-CONCEPT FO URBAN, RURAL AND TRIBAL ADOLESCENTS."

Objectives of the Study

The investigation was carried out with the following objectives:

(i) To study the creative potentiality of urban, rural and tribal adolescents.

(ii) To study the differences in verbal and figural creativity in urban, rural and tribal adolescents.

(iii) To study the sex difference in creativity or urban, rural and tribal adolescents.

(iv) To study the differences in achievement motivation of high and low creative adolescents.

(v) To study the self-concept of high and low creative adolescents.

(vi) To study the relationship between intelligence and creativity.

Hypothessis

Consequent upon research trends (as reported in chapter IV) and objectives of the study, the following hypotheses were formulated for the study:

H_1- There is no significant difference in creative potential in urban, rural and tribal adolescents.

H_2- There is no significant difference in verbal and figural creativity so far as urban, rural and tribal adolescents are concerned.

H_3- There is no significant sex difference in creativity among urban, rural and tribal adolescents.

H_4- There is no significant difference between high and low creative adolescents so far as achievement motivation is concerned.

H_5- There is no significant difference between high and low creative adolescents so far as the self concept is concerned.

H_6- There is no significant relationship between creativity and intelligence.

METHODOLOGY

Design of the Study

The present investigation focuses on comparison between urban, rural and tribal adolescents on their creativity scores. This study also includes variables on achievement motivation, self-concept, urban, rural and tribal background and sex. Intelligence has also been studied in relation to creativity. The study was carried out in the schools of Orissa and the secondary school children formed the major sample of the study.

Sample of the Study

The chief purpose of the present investigation was to study the creative potential of urban, rural and tribal adolescents of western Orissa. The population of the study was secondary school students

(Class IX) of western Orissa. Two things have been taken into consideration by the investigator regarding the quality (representativeness) and quantity (total number) of the sample. The investigator selected four districts of western Orissa namely, Sambalpur, Sundargarh, Bolangir and Kalahandi on the basis of major urban, rural and tribal concentration. The selection of the school from above mentioned districts was purposive. Out of total twenty four schools, there were four boys schools and four girls schools (of urban area) eight co-educational and one girls schools (of rural area); one boys school, four girls school and two co-educational schools (of tribal area). The tribal sample was drawn from school run under Tribal Rural Welfare Scheme (TRW), Govt. of Orissa. On the whole a total of 580 randomly drawn subjects of class IX from urban, rural and tribal areas (204 Ss urban, 213, Ss rural and 163 Ss tribal) constituted the sample of the present study. A detailed picture of the total sample is presented in Table 3.1 and area of sample is located in figure 3.1

Instrument Used:

The following instruments were employed for collection of required data for the present investigation:

(i) Wallach and Kogan Test of Creativity (1956) adopted in Oriya by Tripathy (1979) was employed to assess the creative potential of the subjects.

(ii) Achievement Motivation Test (non-verbal) by Mohan (1971) was employed for the collection of data on achievement motivation (n-Ach.) of the subjects.

(iii) Personality Word List (PWL) by Deo (1971) was employed for assessing the self-concept of the subjects.

(iv) Cattell's culture Fair Test of Intelligence, Form 'A' factor 'g' Scale II (1965) was employed to assess intelligence of the subjects.

ADMINISTRATION OF INSTRUMENTS & SCORING PROCEDURE

The data for the present research work were collected by the investigator personally from the selected schools in Orissa by administering the instruments described above. All the tests were administered during the school hours. The total time taken to administer all the taste in a particular school was three days and the entire data were collected within four months. After administration of the tests, the scoring was done by the investigator in accordance with the scoring procedures prescribed in the respective test manuals. The entire data were scored within next six months by the investigator himself.

STATISTICAL TECHNIQUES EMPLOYED

In the present investigation several statistical techniques were employed to analyse the collected data for major study. According to the nature and complexity of the study to test the various hypotheses based on objectives of the study, different statistical treatments were needed. These techniques are mentioned below:

(i) Descriptive/Inferential Statistical Analysis:

Inferential statistics like means, SD's, 't' ratio, percentiles and testing the significant difference between the means were worked out to compare the groups-urban, rural and tribal on creativity. Percentile techniques was used to identify high creative and low creative groups. Again, SD's, SED, C.R. were used to compare high creative with low creative on achievement motivation and self-concept.

(ii) Correlational Analysis:

The product moment coefficient of correlations were worked out to obtain the nature and the extent of relationship between verbal and figural creativity and non verbal intelligence on urban sample.

Thus, with the help of above statistical treatments the investigate or tests various hypotheses and draws some conclusions thereafter.

CONCLUSIONS (MAIN FINDINGS AND TESTING THE HYPOTHESES)

On the basis of the results obtained during the course of the present study the following conclusions have been drawn. For clarity the conclusions, of the results of this study have been arranged according to the order of the presentation employed in the previous chapter.

Conclusions of Results on Creativity and Culture

Conclusions of Results on Composite Creativity and Cultural Groups:

The results fairly indicate:

(i) Between the urban and rural adolescents, urban adolescents, in general, are more creative than the rural counterparts.

(ii) Between rural and tribal adolescents, tribal adolescents, in general, are more creative than their rural counterparts.

(iii) Between urban and tribal adolescents, both the groups perform same standard. This is to say tribal adolescents, in general, are as creative as their urban counterparts.

Thus, on the basis of the above results, the first hypothesis which states no significant difference among urban, rural and tribal on creative potential got a partial support.

But the hypothesis that there is no significant difference in creative potential between urban and tribal adolescents stands confirmed.

CONCLUSIONS OF RESULTS ON VERBAL/FIGURAL CREATIVITY AND CULTURAL GROUPS:

(i) Urban adolescents are significantly more creative than their rural counterparts on verbal and figural creativity.

(ii) Between rural and tribal adolescents no marked difference is found in respect of the verbal and figural creativity.

(iii) Urban adolescents are more creative than their tribal counterparts on verbal and figural creativity.

Thus, on the basis of above results the second hypothesis that no significant difference exists in verbal and figural creativity of urban, rural and tribal adolescents got a partial support in the study.

The hypothesis of no difference was only proved in case of rural and tribal adolescents in verbal and figural creativity. Here particularly in this case our null hypothesis got a full support.

CONCLUSIONS OF RESULTS ON SEX DIFFERENCES IN CREATIVITY IN DIFFERENT CULTURAL GROUPS:

(i) Among the urban adolescents urban girls are found to be significantly more creative than urban boys in all verbal, figural and composite creativity.
(ii) Among rural adolescents, rural boys are found to by significantly more creative than rural girls in verbal and composite creativity, but in figural creativity rural girls are equally creative as their rural boys.
(iii) Among the tribal adolescents tribal boys are more creative than tribal girls in figural and composite creativity. But in verbal creativity tribal girls are equally creative as tribal boys.

Thus, on the basis of the above results the third hypothesis that the existence of no sex difference in urban, rural and tribal adolescents in verbal, figural and composite creativity got partial support in the study. As the above results indicate the hypothesis of no sex difference got full support in case of rural boys and girls on figural creativity and in tribal boys and girls on verbal creativity.

However, the evidence of inter-group sex difference in respect of composite, verbal, figural creativity will be quite informative, stimulating and promising. The conclusions of the results of inter-group sex difference in respect of different components of creativity are given as under:

(i) Urban boys are more creative than rural girls in composite creativity.
(ii) Urban girls are more creative than rural boys in composite creativity.
(iii) Urban girls are more creative than rural girls in composite creativity.
(iv) Tribal boys are more creative than rural girls in composite creativity.
(v) Tribal girls are more creative than rural girls in composite creativity.
(vi) Tribal boys are more creative than rural girls in composite creativity.
(vii) Urban girls are more creative than tribal boys in composite creativity.
(viii) Urban girls are more creative than rural girls in composite creativity.
(ix) Urban boys are more creative than rural girls in verbal creativity.

(x) Urban girls are more creative than rural girls in verbal creativity.

(xi) Urban girls are more creative than rural boys in verbal creativity.

(xii) Tribal boys are more creative than rural girls in verbal creativity.

(xiii) Tribal girls are more creative than rural girls in verbal creativity.

(xiv) Urban girls are more creative than tribal girls in verbal creativity.

(xv) Urban girls are more creative than tribal boys in verbal creativity.

(xvi) Rural boys are more creative than urban boys in figural creativity.

(xvii) Urban girls are more creative than rural boys in figural creativity. (xviii) urban girls are more creative than rural girls in figural creativity.

(xix) Tribal boys are more creative than rural boys in figural creativity.

(xx) Rural boys are more creative than tribal girls in figural creativity.

(xxi) Tribal boys are more creative than rural girls in figural creativity.

(xxii) Tribal boys are more creative than urban boys in figural creativity.

(xxiii) Urban girls are more creative than tribal boys in figural creativity.

(xxiv) Urban girls are more creative than tribal girls in figural creativity.

Thus, out of total 36 inter-group comparable pairs significant inter-group sex differences were found in 24 pairs mentioned above. However, 12 pairs did not differ significantly. The pairs that did not differ significantly are: urban boys and rural boys, rural boys and tribal boys rural boys and tribal girls, urban boys bad tribal girls in composite creativity; urban boys and rural boys rural boys and tribal boys, rural boys and tribal girls, urban boys and tribal boys, urban boys and tribal girls in verbal creativity; urban boys and rural girls, rural girls and tribal girls, urban boys and tribal girls in figural creativity respectively. Thus the hypothesis of no sex difference is partially supported by the results of the study.

CONCLUSIONS OF RESULTS ON CREATIVITY AND ACHIEVEMENT MOTIVATION

(i) High creative urban adolescents, as compared to low creative urban adolescents, in general, possess higher achievement motivation or greater achievement need.

(ii) High creative rural adolescents as compared to low creative rural adolescents, in general, possess greater achievement need.

(iii) High creative tribal adolescents as compared to low creative tribal adolescents, in general, possess greater need achievement.

Thus, on the basis of above results the 4th hypothesis that states no significant difference exists between the high creative and low creative so far as achievement motivation is concerned is fully rejected. Results of the study clearly states that there exists marked differences between high creative and low creative so far as achievement motivation is concerned.

CONCLUSIONS OF RESULTS ON CREATIVITY AND ACHIEVEMENT MOTIVATION

(i) The perceived self-concept of high creative urban adolescents as compared to low creative urban adolescents, in general, is significantly higher.

(ii) The perceived self-concept of high creative rural adolescents as compared to low creative rural adolescents, in general, is significantly higher.

(iii) The perceived self-concept of high creative tribal adolescents do not differ markedly. In other words perceived self-concept of low creative tribal adolescents is as higher as their high creative counterparts.

Thus, on the basis of the above results the 5th hypothesis that states no significant difference exist between high creative and low creative self-concept wise is partially accepted. Results of the study clearly state that there exists marked differences between high creative and low creative so far as self-concept of urban and rural subjects are concerned. Where as among the tribal subjects high creative do not differ from low creative self-conceptualise.

CONCLUSIONS OF RESULTS ON CREATIVITY AND SELF-CONCEPT

(i) The relationship between verbal creativity and intelligence is significant but low.
(ii) The relationship between figural creativity and intelligence is significant but low.
(iii) The relationship between composite creativity and intelligence is significant but low.

Thus, on the basis of the above results the 6th hypothesis that states 'no relationship' between creativity and intelligence in fully rejected. Result of the study clearly states that there exists positive relationship (though low) between components of creativity and intelligence.

Bibliography

Agarwal, P.C. (1974). A study of the achievement motive, Unpublished Ph.D. thesis, Education, K.U.K.

Ahmad, S.I. (1977). A study of certain Creativity factors among school children, *Psychological Studies*, 22,24-27.

Allport G.W. (1961). *Pattern of Growth in Personality*. New York : Holt.

Anastasi, A. (1949) : *Differential Psychology* New York : Macmilllan in 1958; earlier edition, 1949.

Anastasi, A. and Schaefer, C.E. (1971). Notes on the Concepts of Creativity and Intelligence. *Journal of Creative Behaviour*, 5(2), 113-16.

Anderson, J.F. (1960). The Nature of Abilities. In E.P. Torrance (*Education and Talent*. Minnesota : University of Minnesota Press, Minnesota.

Anderson, H.N. and Anderson, G.L. (1961). Across-national Study in Creativity and Mental health. (Paper presented at the Sixth International Congress on Mental Health, Technical Section August 31, 1961.

Anderson, J. *et al* (1970). *Thesis and Assignment Writing*. New Delhi: Wiley Eastern Limited.

Ariestis, S. (1976), *Creativity* : The Magic Synthesis, NYC : Basic Books.

Atkinson, J.W. (1958) *A theory of Achievement Motivation*. New York John wiley and Sons.

Azmi A.A. (1974). A study of the Relationship between Creativity, Culture and Intelligence among Middle School Rural Children, Unpublished Master's thesis A.M.U.

Bandrinath, S. and Satyanarayan, S.B. (1979). Correlates of creative thinking of high school students. Creativity News Letter 7(2) 16-23.

Barron, Frank (1963). Creativity and Psychological health, (2nd ed.) Princeton, New Jersey Van Nostrand.

Barron F. (1965). The Psychology of Creativity

Baron, F.X. (1969). Creative Person and Creative Process. New York: Halt, Rinchart Winston.

Barrown, F and Harrington, D.M. (1981). Creativity, Intelligence and Personality. Annual Review of Psychology, 32, 439-76.

Best J.W. (1977). Research in Education. New Delhi : Prentice Hall of India.

Bhan, R.N. (1972) Social factors in Creative Potentiality, Journal of Education and Psychology, 29,263-67.

Blatt, S.J. and Stein, M.I. (1957). Some Personality Values and Cognitive Characteristics of Creative Person. American Journal of Psychology 12.

Bloom B.S. (1963). Report on creativity research by the examiners Office of the University of Chicago. In C.W. Taylor and F. Barron Eds. Scientific Creativity. Its recognition and development. Teachers College Bursaw & Publication.

Buch M.B. (Ed.) 1974-78. Second survey of research in education Baroda : Society for Educational Research and Development, 1979.

Buch, M.B.(Ed) 1978-1983. *Third Survey of research in education*. New Delhi : National Council of Educational Research & Training, 1987.

Burt, C. (1962). The Psychology of Creative Ability. British *Journal of Educational Psychology* 32,292-98.

Butter, J.M. and Haigh, G.S. (1954). Changes in the relation between self-concepts and ideal concepts consequent upon client centred counselling In C.R. Rogers and R.P. Dynona (Eds.) *Psycho-therapy and Personality Change, Chicago*: University of Chicago.

Cattell, R.B. (1965). Cattall's culture Fair Test of Intelligence, Factor 'G' Form 'A' Psychological Corporation of India, Agra.

Chadha, M.K. (1987). Creativity as a function of intelligence, Personality, Scholastic achievement : An Empirical Study. *Indian Educational Review* XXII (1) 61-64.

Chhotu Ram (1979). A factorial study of the measures of Self-concept, motivation and projective and Psychometric measure of Personality, Master's thesis, Psychology, K.U.K.

Clark, C.M. *et al* (1965) Convergent and Divergent Thinking Abilities of Talented Adolescents. *Journal of Educational Psychology*, 56(3), 157-163.

Craig, R.H. (1966). Traits, Tests and Creativity, Psychologia: *International Journal of Psychology*, 9,107-110.

Croplsy A.J. (1966). Creativity and Intelligence, *British Journal of Educational Psychology*, 36,259-66.

—— (1967). Creativity, Intelligence and Achievement. *Journal of Educational Research* 13(1) 51-58.

Cropley A.J. (1968). A note on the Wallach Kogan tests of creativity, *British Journal of Psychology*, 38,197-201.

—— (1980) Research on measurement of creativity. In M.K. Raina (Ed.) *Creativity Research: International Perspective*, New Delhi : National Council of Educational Research and Training.

Croplsy A.J. and Maslancy, G.W. (1969) Reliability and factorial validity of Wallach Kogan Tests. *British Journal of Psychology*, 60, 365-78.

Damm, V.J. (1970) Creativity and Intelligences : Research implications for equal emphasis in high School. *Exceptional Children*, 36, 565-70.

Dellas, M. and Gaier, E.L. (1970). Identification of creativity: The individual, *Psychological Bulletin*, 73(1), 55-73.

Dan, Prativa (1971). "Personality word List" - A self Rating Scale developed in the Deptt. of Education, Punjab University, Chandigarh.

Deshmukh, M.N. (1979) An Analytical Study of Some Scholastic Conditions and Practices as Contributory Factors to Creative ability. Ph.D. thesis, Education Nagpur University.

Dey P. (1986). Measurement of creative ability. An investigation, *Indian Educational Review*, XXI (1), 68-75.

Dhaliwal, A.S. (1984) Why and How to Identify and Nurture the Creative Minority. *Personality study and Group Behaviour*, 4(2), 73-85.

Dharmanganda, B. (1981). Creativity in relation to sex, age and locale, *Psychologial Studies*, 26,28-33.

Dhir, S. (1973). Performance of High School Students on Verbal and Figural Tests of Creative Thinking. Master's thesis, Punjab University.

Drevdanl, J.E. and Cattell, R.B. (1958) Personality and Creativity in Artists and Writers. *Journal of Clinical Psychology*, 14. 107-11.

Dutta G. (1982) Sex Difference in Creativity Among the Tribal of Meghalaya, *Journal of Institute of Educational Research* 6(2), 23-26.

Dutta, M.L. (1983) Achievement Motive : A Conceptual Framework. *Journal of Indian Education* - IX (4) 33-36.

Edqards, A.L. (1971). *Experimental Design in Psychological Research*, New Delhi : Amerind Publishing Co. Pvt.. Ltd.

Eisenman, R. and Robinson, M. (1964). Complexity-Simplicity, Creativity, Intelligence and Other correlates, *Journal of Psychology*, 67(2), 331-334.

Fee. F. (1968). An alternative towards factor analysis of Wallachkogan's creativity correlation. *British Journal of Educational Psychology*.

Foster, J. (1971) *Creativity and the teacher*. London : Macmllan.

Freedom, J. *et at* (1968) Creativity : A Selective Review of Research (2nd Ed) London : Society for research into Higher Education.

Gakhar, Sudesh K. (1981). Intellectual and Personality Correlates of Creativity. *Indian Dissertation Abstract*, v. (344) 332-34.

Gardner, J.W. (1961). Excellence, New York : Harper and Roe.

Garrett, H.E. and Woodworth, R.S. (1971). Statistics in Psychology and Education. Bombay. Vakils, Feffer, and Simons Pvt. Ltd.

Getzels, J.W. and Jackson, P.W. (1959). Highly Intellective and Highly Creative Adolescents. A summary of some research findings. In the third University of Utha. Research conference on the Identification of Creative Scientific Talent.

—— (1962) Creativity and intelligence. New York : John wilay and Sons, Inc.

Ghiselin, B. (Ed.) 1952. The creative process : A symposium Barkeley, Calif : University of California Press.

Ghiselin, B. (1966). Ultimate criteria for two levels of creativity. In C.W. Taylor and F. Borrown (Eds) Scientific Creativity : Its Recognition and Development. New York: John wiley and Sons, 30-43.

Gokulananthan, P.P. and Mehta, P. (1972). Achievement Motive in Tribal and Non-verbal Assamese Secondary School Adolescents. *Indian Educational Review* 7(1).

Ginsberg, G.P. and Whitemore, R.G. (1968) Creativity and Ability: A Direct Observation of their Relationship. *British Journal of Educational Psychology*, 38 133-139.

Good C.V. (1973) *Dictionary of Education*. New York : McGraw Hill Book co-Inc.

Gordon, W.J.J. (1961). Synetiics: The Development of Creative Capacity. New York : Harper and Row.

Gordon, J.C. (1967) Creativity : Its Educational Implications. New York : John Wiley and Sons.

—— (1972) Development of the creative individual. San Diego, Calif : Robert, R. Knapp.

Gowan J.C. and Dison, M. (1979). The Society which Maximises Creativity. *Journal of Creative Behaviour* 13(3), 194-210.

Goyal, R.P. (1974) Creativity and Sex Differences: An overview of research findings. *Creativity Newsletter*, 75, 243-44.

Guilford, J.P. (1950) Creativity: *American Psychologist*, 2, 444-54.

—— (1956) The structure of Intellect. *Psychologial Bulletin*, 53, 267-93.

—— (1959) Traits of Creativity. In H.H. Anderson (Ed.) *Creativity and its Cultivation*. New York: Harper and Row.

—— (1962) Creativity : Its Measurement and Development. In S.J. Parnes and H.F. Harding (Eds.) : *A source Book for creative thinking*. 156-68.

—— (1967) Creativity : Yesterday, To-day and Tomorrow. *Journal of Creative Behaviour*, 1,3-14.

—— (1968). *Intelligence, Creativity and their Educational Implication*. San Disgo California : Robert R. Knapp.

—— (1969). Some Theoretical View of Creativity. In H. Halson and W. Bevan's (Eds.) *Contemporary Approach to Psychology*. New Delhi: Affiliated East West Press.

—— (1970). Creativity : Retrospect and Prospect, *Journal of Creative Behaviour*, 493), 149-68.

—— (1973). An Informational Theory of Creative Thinking. Educational Trends, 8(1-4), 1-6.

Gulati, Sushma (1982). A Study of the Analysis and Synthesis of Creativity. *Indian Educational Review*, 17(1), 104-08.

Gupta, A.K. (1980). A Factorial Study of Verbal and Non-verbal Creativity, Intelligence and Socio-economic Status, Model Institute of Educational Research, Jammu.

Gupta A.K. and Sharma S.K. (1977). A Study of Institutional Climate and Teaching Verbal Behaviour in Relation to Creativity. ICSSR Project, New Delhi.

Haimowitz, N.R. and Haimuwitz, M.L. What Makes Them Creative? In M.L. Haimowitz and N.R. Haimowitz (Eds.) *Human Development : Selected Reading* New York : Tomas Y. Crowell Co .44-55.

Hall, G.S. and Lindzey, G. (1957). *Theories of Personality*. London : John Wiley and Sons.

Hassan, P. and Butcher, H.J. (1966). Creativity and intelligence : A Partial Replication with Scottish Children of Gatzels and Jackson Study. *British Journal of Psychology*, 57, 122-33.

Hattle J.A. (1980 B) Should Creativity be Administered under Test like Conditions ? An Empirical Study of Alternative Conditions *Journal of Educational Psychology*, 72, 99-98.

Hattie, J.A. and Rogers, H.J. (1986) Factor Models for Assessing the Relationship Between Creativity and Intelligence. *Journal of Educational Psychology*, 78 (6), 482-485.

Hota, A.K. (1982) Search for Talent, *Indian Education* 12(1 & 2) 62-65.

—— (1983) Nurturing Non-academic Talent in the School : A Challenge *Journal of Indian Edn.* 8(6) 35-41.

Hota A.K. (1984) Creativity ; As It Seems To Be. *The Education Quarterly* 36(1) 46-50.

—— (1985) Teachability and Creativity *Aukura*, 1, 1-10.

—— (1987 a) Do Parents Make Any Difference? A Cognitive Approach. *Parents and Children*, XXIV (5) 9-11.

—— (1987 a). Sishura Srujani Shaktira Bikash Pain Amar Daitva (Oriya). All India Radio Sambalpur 11th Apr. 1987.

—— (1987 b) Navodaya Vidyalaya O Palil Prativa (Oriya) Utkal Prasanga, Vol .43 (182) 42-43.

—— (1987 C). Sishu Srujana Shilati Vikashra Ketoti diga (Oriya) Pourusha, 21(5) 37-40.

—— (1988 a). Guidance Beyond School, (Paper Presented in Refresher course in Guidance, NCERT New Delhi, 27th to 29th January, 1988.

Hudosn, L. (1966). Contrary Imagination, London : Methuen.

—— (1966). Intelligence : Convergent & Divergent. Penguin science Survey.

Hurlock, E.B. (1974). *Personality Development*. New York: Mac. Graw Hill.

Hussain, M.G. (1974). Creativity and Sex Differences, *Psychological Studies* 19, 127-29.

Jarial, G.S. (1982). Relation between Creativity and Intelligence: A Review, *ISPT Journal of Research* VI, 1-8.

Hussian, M. *et al* (1975). Cultural roles, sex differences and creativity. *Educational Trends*, 10(2), 141-45.

Jawa, S. (1971). Creativity as Related to Achievements Motivation and Birth Order. *Indian Psychological Review* 7, 24-26.

Jawa S. (1974). A study of creativity and some of its Personality and Environmental Correlates, Unpublished, Ph.D. Thesis, Delhi University.

Jha, S.K. (1978) *An analysis of certain dimensions of creativity*. Bombay: Himalaya Pub. House.

Keer, W.A. and Abraham P. (1962). Halstead Brain Impairment, Boldness, Creativity and Group Intelligence. *Journal of Clinical Psychology*, 80,259-266.

Kalman H. (1971). *Helping People*, New York : Science House.

Khire U-(1971). Creativity in relation to Intelligence and Personality factors, Unpublished Doctoral thesis, poona University , Poona.

Kishore, G. (1981) A Developmental Study of Creativity in Relation to Certain Personality Correlates. Ph.D. Psychol. Aligarh Muslim University.

Kneller, G.F. (1965) *The Art and Science of Creativity*. New York: Halt, Rinehart and winston.

Kogan, Nathan (1974). *Configuration of Cultural Growth*. Berkeley: University of California press.

Kubie L. (1958). *Neurotic Distortion of the Creative Process*.

Lawrence : University of Kansas Press.

Kumar G. (1978). Creative functioning in relation to Personality, Value orientation and Achievement motivation. *Indian Educational Review, XIII* (2), 110-15.

LOEVINGER, J. (1966). The Meaning and Measurement of Ago Development. *American Psychologist*, 21, 195-206.

Mac Kinnon, J.W. (1962). The Nature and Nurture of Creative Talent. *American Psychologist*, 17 484-95.

—— (1968) Psychologist Aspects of Creativity. In D.W. still (Ed.)

International Encyclopedia of the Social Science. London : Macmillan and Free Press 3, 435-41.

—— (1970). Creativity : A Multifaceted Phenomenon. In John D. Roslanskey (ed.). *Creativity*. Amstardom : North Holland pub. Co.

Mc Candless, B. (1952). Relation of Environmental Factors to Intellectual Functioning. In H.H. Stevens and R. Herber (ed) *Mantal Ratetardation*. Chicago : University of Chicago Press, 175-213.

Mc Clelland, D.C. (1958) Methods of Measuring Human Motivation. In J.W. Atkinson (Ed.) *Moties in Fantesy Action and Society*, D. Van Nostrand Co. Inc. 7-42.

—— (1964) The Roots of Consciousness: Ivan Nostrand Co .Mc. 44-45.

Mc Clelland, D.C. at al (1953). *The Achievement Motive*, New York : Appleton Countering Crofts.

Mc Clelland D.C. *et al* (1953). A Scoring Manual for the Achievement Motive. In Atkinson J.W. *et al Motives in Fantasy, Action and Society*, 179-204.

Mc Kinney, James J., and Forman, S.C. (1977). Factor Structure of wallack-Kogan Test of Creativity and Measures of Intelligence and Achievement. *Psychology in School* 14(3), 41-44.

Maltzman, I.et at (1958). A Procedure for Increasing word Association Originality and its Transfer Effect. *Journal of Exceptional Psychology*, 56, 392-98.

Maltzman, I. *et al* (1960). On the Training of Originality. *Psychological Review*, 67(4) 229-42.

Mari, S.K. (1971). Creativity of American and Arab Rural Youth: A Cross-cultural Study. *Doctoral Dissertation*, University of Winconsin.

Maslow, A.H. (1954) Motivation and Personality New York : Harpers and Row.

—— (1959) Creativity in self Actualizing People. An Anderson, H.A. (Ed.) *Creativity and its Cultivation*. New York : Harper Brothers.

May R. (1959) The Nature of Creativity. In H.H. Anderson (Ed.) Creativity and its Cultivation. New York : Harper Brothers.

Mead, M (1959), Creativity in Cross-cultural Perspective. In Anderson, H.H. (Ed.) *Creativity and its cultivation*. 233.

Mead, M., and Metranx, R. (1953). The Study of Culture at Distance. Chicago : University of Chicago press.

Mednick S.A. (1962). The Associative Basis of the Creative Process. Psychological Review, 69,220-32.

Mehdi, B. (1973). A Quick Screening Device for Identifying the Creative Personality. Creativity News letter 4, 45-48.

—— (1974). Creativity, Intelligence and Achievement Some Findings of recent research. Indian Educational Review 9(1).

—— (1977) Creativity, Intelligence and Achievement: A Correlational Study, Psychologial Studies 22(1), 55-62.

Mehdi, B(Ed) 1977. Creativity in Teaching and Learning Measure: Regional College of Education.

Milgram, R.M. *et al* (1987) Original Thinking in Israeli Pre-school Children, School Psychology 8(1), 54-58.

Mishra, R.G. *et at* (1981). Studies on National Talent Search (Manograph). New Delhi : NCERT.

Mohan, Asha (1971). Test of Achievement Motivation (n-Ach.) Developed according to Mc Clealland Pattern. Psychological Corporation, Agra.

Mooney, R.L. (1963) A Conceptual Model for Integrating Four Approaches to the Identification of Creative Talent. In C.W. Taylor and F. Barron (ed) *Scientific Creativity. Its recognition and development*. New York : John Willey & Sons.

Moran, J.D. *et al* (1983) Original Thinking in Pre-school Children. Child Development 54, 921-26.

Morgan, W *et al* (1980). Conjecturing About Creative Leaders. Journal of Creative Behaviour, 14(4) 225-34.

Muddu V. (1980) A study of some Personality Correlates of Intelligence and Creative Abilities Among High School Students in Andhra Predesh, Ph.D. Education, Osmania University.

Murphy, H.A. (1938). Explorations in Personality. New York : Oxford University Press Inc.

Nash P. (1966) Authority and Freedom in Education, New York : John Wiley and Sons.

Osborn, A.F. (1953). Applied Imagination. New York : Scribners.

Page, G.T. and Thomas, J.R. (1977). International Dictionary of Education Kogan Page, London : Nicols Publishing Co.

Pandey R.C. and Pandey R.N. (1984). A Study of Creativity in relation to Sex of High School Students. *Indian Psychological Review*, 26(2), 53-57.

Paramesh C.R. (1969). A study of Creativity in Relation to Extraversion, Emotionality, Body Image and Values, Ph.D. Dissertation, Madras University, Madras.

—— (1970) Value Orientation of Creative Person, *Psychological Studies*, 15(2), 108-112.

Parroff, M.S. and Dutta, L.E. (1965). Personality Characteristics of the Potential creative scientists, Socio-Psycho *Analysis*, 8. 91-106.

Passi, B.K. (1971). An Exploratory Study of Creativity and its Relationship with Intelligence and Achievement in School Subjects at Higher Secondary Stage. Ph.D. Thesis, Punjab University.

Parnes, S.J. (1967). Creative Behaviour Guide Book. New York: Charles Scribner's Sons.

Passi, B.K. and Lalithama, M.S. (1973), Self Concept and Creativity of Over, Normal and Underachieving Amongst Grade Students of Borada. *Indian Journal of Psychology & Education* 4,1-11.

Pathak, P.A. (1962). Expiratory Study of Creativity, Intelligence and School Achievement. Psychological studies. 7, 1-9.

Persaud, G. and Stimpson A. (1986). Creative thinking and non-verbal I.Q. among three grades of school children, Journal of Creative Behaviour, 20(2), 146.

Poincare, H. (1972). Mathematical Creation, In P.E. Vernon (Ed) Creativity. Harmods worth: Penguin Books 77-88.

Qureshi A.N. (1980). A Study of Creativity in Relation to Intelligence, Manifest Anxiety and Level of Aspiration of High School Girls, Ph.D. Psychology, Agra University.

Raina M.K. (1968) A study of some correlates of creativity in Indian students. Unpublished Doctoral thesis, Rajasthan University.

—— (1969) Creativity: research in India : Analysis. Journal of Creative Behaviour 3,111-14.

—— (1969) Sex Difference and Creativity. *Psychological Studies*, 19(2), 127-29.

—— (1980) Creativity Research; *International Perspective* New Delhi: N C E R T.

Raina, T.N. (1982). Sex Difference in Creativity in India : A second look. Indian Educational Review, 17,122-28.

Raj H.S.S. (1978). The Overlap of Creativity with Certain Cognitive and Affective Variables. Ph.D. Kerala University.

Rajput A.S. (1984) Study of Academic Achievement of Student in Mathematics in Relation to their Intelligence, Achievement Motivation and Socio-economic Status. Unpublished Ph.D. thesis, Punjab University. Chandigarh.

Rewat, M.S. and Agarwal, S. (1977). A Study of Creative Thinking with Reference to Intelligence, Sex, Community, and Income Groups. *Indian Psychological Review*, 14(2).

Report of the Secondary Education Commission (1952-53).

Report of the Education Commission (1966)

Richard, J.K. and Needham, W.C. *et al* (1963). Creativity Test and Teacher and Self Rating Originality. Journal of Experimental Education 32(3) 281-85.

Richardson, A.G. (1986) Sex Difference in Creativity Among Jamaican Adolescents Journal of Creative Behaviour, 20,(2), 147.

Ripple R.L. and May, F. (1962). Caution in Comparing Creativity and I.Q. Psychological Report, 10,229-230.

Rogers C. (1959). Towards a Theory of Creativity. In H.H. Anderson (Ed) Creativity and its Cultivation, New York: Harper and Brothers, 69-82.

Rogers, C.R. (1961). Towards a Theory of Creativity. In C. Rogers (Ed) On becoming a person Boston: Houghton, Mifflin, 1961.

Sansanwal D.N. and Jarral G.S. (1987) Creativity and its Components in relation to different level of Intelligence and academic subjects among high school students. Journal of Educational Research and Extension 23(3), 122-28.

Sapir, E. (1934). The Emergence of the Concept of Personality in a Study of Cultures. *Journal of Social Psychology* 5, 408-15.

Saxena S. (1981). A study of need achievement in relation to Creativity, Values, Level of Aspiration and Anxiety, *Ph.D. Education*, Agra University.

Schlit, W.H. (1968). Creativity and Intelligence ; Further findings *Journal of Clinical Psychological* 24 (4), 458.

Shanker, B.R. (1974). Cultural Barriers to Creativity. Creativity Newsletter, 3(1) 25.

Sharma K.N. (1972), Creativity as a Function of Intelligence. *Psychological Studies*, 17 (1 & 2) 64-67.

—— (1972) Rural urban difference in creative thinking. Journal of Psychological Research 16(3), 121-22.

—— (1974). Creativity as a function of Intelligence. Interest and Culture. Creativity Newsletter 3, 30-37.

Shukla J.P. and Sharma V.P. (1987). A Cross Cultural Study of Scientific Creativity. Indian Journal of Applied Psychology 24(2) 101-06.

Shukla, P.C. (1982). A Study of Creativity in Relation to Sex Locality and School Subject. Indian Educational Review, 17,2,128-32.

Singh A. (1978). Is Intelligence Inherited? New Delhi : National Council of Educational Research and Training.

Singh R.B. (1977) Creativity as related to intelligence, achievement and Security -Insecurity, *Indian Psychological Review*, 14,(2).

Singh R.G. *et al* (1977) Creativity as Related to Intelligence : *Indian Psychological Review*, 14,2,14-18.

Singh R.J. (1978) Challenges and Issues in Measurement of Creativity. *Indian Journal of Psychometry and Education*. 9(1), 15-20.

—— (1985). Creativity - A Socio Psychological Interpretation. National Journal of Education. VII, (2), 17-24.

Singh S. and Mahra, P.G. (1982). A Correlational Study of Intelligence and Various Comments of Creativity, ISPT *Journal of Research* VI, 15-21.

Singh S.P. (1970). Creative Abilities : A Cross Cultural Study Journal of Social Psychology 81, 125-26.

Spearman, C.W. (1930) Creative Mind. London : Cambridge University Press.

Stein, M.I. and Heinze, S.J. (1960). Creativity and the Individual New York.

Strauss, J.M. and Strauss, M.A. (1968). Family Roles and Sex Differences in Creativity of Children in Bombay and Minnepolis *Journal of Marriage and Family Life*, 30, 46-53.

Suess, E.F. (1981). The Influence of Differential Acculturation on the Creativity of Alaskan Eskimb Middle School Students. Doctoral Dissertation, United States of International University.

Taft, R. *et al* (1970). Creative Attitudes and Creative Productivity: A Comparison of two Aspects of Creativity Among Students Journal of Educational Psychology 61, 136-43

Tara S.N. (1981). Sex Difference in Creativity Among Early Adolescents in India. Perceptual and Motor skills 52, 959-62.

Taylor C.W. (1964). Creativity Progress and Potential New York: Mc Graw Hill Book Co.

—— (1964) Widening Horizons on Creativity. New York. Boston; Honghton Rofflin.

Thakaran, P.N.O. (1987). The Effect of Rural and Urban Upringing on Congnitive Styles Psychological Studies 32,2, 119-22.

Tichor, M.I. (1973), Culture and Creativity in M.A. Coler (ed). *Essarys on Creativity in Science*. New York University Press.

Torrance E.P. (1960) Talent and Education Minnepolis : Minnesota University Press.

Torrance E.P. (1962). Guiding Creative Talent. Eagle wood cliffs, J.J. Apprentice Hall Inc.

—— (1965) Rewarding Creative Behaviour. Englewood Cliffs, N.J. Prentice Hall.

—— (1966), Torrance Test of Creative Thinking : Norms technical manual (research edition). Princeton NJ : Personal Press.

Torrance, E.P. (1987). Nurturing creative talents - Theory into Practice 5, 168-74.

—— (1969). Comparative studies of creativity in children. Educational Leadership 27, 146-48.

—— (1970) Encouraging Creativity in Class Room. Dubuque Lowa; Brown

Tripathy, S. (1979). Wallach and Kogan Test of Creativity; its Oriya adoptation, Deptt. of Education, Kurukshetra University, Kurukshetra.

Uzgirls, I.C (1968) Socio-cultural Factors in Cognitive Development. (Paper Presented at the peadody NIMH conference on socio-cultural aspect of mental retardation, Nushevelle, Tennesses, 10-12.

Vessesi, Rama (1985). Cognite Style, Needs and Values of High and Low Creative Adolescents. Unpublished Ph.D. Thesis Punjab University, Chandigarh.

Veevan R.C. and Smith, B.G. 1967 Motivation and Achievement Motivation. Mc Graw Hill Book Co.

Vernon, P.E. (1971) Effects of Administration and Scoring Divergent Thinking Tests. British Journal of Educational Psychology 1, 245-57.

——(Ed.) 1972. Creativity Harondoworth: Pengian Books Vervalin, C.H. (1971). Just What is Creativity ? In G.A. Davis and J.A. Scott *Training Creative Thinking*, New York; Holt, Rinchrt winston, 59-63.

Vessels, G. (1982) The Creative Process An Open System Conceptualization. *Journal of Creative Behaviour*. 16 (3) 185-96.

Wallach, M.A. and Kogan, N. (1963). Wallach Kogan Test of Creativity.

——(1965) Modes of Thinking in Young Children: *A survey of creativity intelligence distinction*. New York; Holt, Rinehart and Winston.

——(1965) A New Look at Creativity Intelligence Distinction. *Journal of personality*, 33, 348-69.

Wallach M.A. and Wing, C.W.Jr. (1969). *The talented students : A Validation of the Creativity Intelligence Distinction*. New York; Holt, Rinehart and Winston.

Wellas, G (1926). The art of thought . London: Jonasthan Cape, New York: Harcourt Brace.

Ward J. (1967). An Oblique Facorization of Wallach and Kogan's Creativity Correlations. *British Journal of Educational Psychology*, 37, 380-82.

Ward W.C. and Cox, P.W. (1974) A Field Study of Non-verbal Creativity. Journal of Personality 42 (2) 202-19

Wechsler, D. (1958) Measurement and Appraisal of Adult Intelligence. New York Williams & Wilkins.

Weisberg, P.S. and Springer, K.J. (1961). Environmental Factors in Creativity Functioning. *Archives of General Psychatry*.

Witkin, H.A. (1967) A Cognitive Style Approach to Cross Cultural Research. *International Journal of Psychology*, 2, 223-50.

Yadav .RS. (1985) A Correlational Study of Intelligence, Age, Academic Achievement and Parental Income of High School Science Students. *Indian Educational Review*.

——(1987) Correlation Among Intelligence, Academic Achievement and Creativity. *The Progress of Education* LX1 (10-11) 218-21.

Yamamota, K.K. (1964). Threshold of Intelligence in Academic Achievement of High Creative Students. *Journal of Experimental Education* 32, 401-05.

Zargar, 4.H. (1980) As Study of Expression, Neuroticism and Achievement in Relation to Intelligence, Creativity and Scholastic Achievement. Ph.D. Education Kashmir University.

Index